Overcoming Common Problems

COPING WITH DEPRESSION AND ELATION

Dr Patrick McKeon

M.D., M.R.C.P.I., M.R.C. Psych.

SHELDON PRESS
LONDON

First published in Great Britain in 1986 by
Sheldon Press, SPCK, Marylebone Road, London NW1 4DU

Fourth Impression 1989

British Library Cataloguing in Publication Data

McKeon, Patrick
    Coping with depression and elation.—(Overcoming
common problems)
    1. Depression, Mental
    I. Title   II. Series
    616.85'27   RC537

ISBN 0-85969-502-6
ISBN 0-85969-503-4 Pbk

Typeset by Delatype, Ellesmere Port
Printed in Great Britain by
Whitstable Litho Ltd, Whitstable, Kent

COPING WITH DEPRESSION AND ELATION

DR PATRICK McKEON is Consultant Psychiatrist at
St Patrick's Hospital, Dublin. He studied at University
College, Dublin, and is a Member of the Royal College
of Physicians of Ireland, the Royal Irish Academy of
Medicine and the Royal College of Psychiatrists. He is
also a Clinical Teacher at Dublin University. Dr
McKeon has published a number of articles on depression and obsessive-compulsive neurosis, and is co-author
of *Multiple Choice Questions in Psychiatry* (Pitman,
1985). He has a special interest in the treatment of
depression and elation, and runs a mood disorder
therapeutic programme. He is currently researching
resistant depression.

Overcoming Common Problems Series

The ABC of Eating
Coping with anorexia, bulimia and
compulsive eating
JOY MELVILLE

An A–Z of Alternative Medicine
BRENT Q. HAFEN AND KATHRYN J.
FRANDSEN

Arthritis
Is your suffering really necessary?
DR WILLIAM FOX

Being the Boss
STEPHEN FITZSIMON

Birth Over Thirty
SHEILA KITZINGER

Body Language
How to read others' thoughts by their gestures
ALLAN PEASE

Calm Down
How to cope with frustration and anger
DR PAUL HAUCK

Comfort for Depression
JANET HORWOOD

Common Childhood Illnesses
DR PATRICIA GILBERT

Complete Public Speaker
GILES BRANDRETH

Coping with Depression and Elation
DR PATRICK McKEON

Coping Successfully with Your Child's Asthma
DR PAUL CARSON

Coping Successfully with Your Child's Skin
Problems
DR PAUL CARSON

Coping Successfully with Your Hyperactive
Child
DR PAUL CARSON

Curing Arthritis Cookbook
MARGARET HILLS

Curing Arthritis – The Drug-free Way
MARGARET HILLS

Curing Illness – The Drug-free Way
MARGARET HILLS

Depression
DR PAUL HAUCK

Divorce and Separation
ANGELA WILLANS

The Epilepsy Handbook
SHELAGH McGOVERN

Everything You Need to Know about Adoption
MAGGIE JONES

Everything You Need to Know about Contact
Lenses
DR ROBERT YOUNGSON

Everything You Need to Know about the
Pill
WENDY COOPER AND TOM SMITH

Everything You Need to Know about Shingles
DR ROBERT YOUNGSON

Family First Aid and Emergency Handbook
DR ANDREW STANWAY

Feverfew
A traditional herbal remedy for migraine and
arthritis
DR STEWART JOHNSON

Fight Your Phobia and Win
DAVID LEWIS

Flying Without Fear
TESSA DUCKWORTH AND DAVID
MILLER

Goodbye Backache
DR DAVID IMRIE WITH COLLEEN
DIMSON

Good Publicity Guide
REGINALD PEPLOW

Helping Children Cope with Grief
ROSEMARY WELLS

How to Be Your Own Best Friend
DR PAUL HAUCK

How to Control your Drinking
DRS W. MILLER AND R. MUNOZ

Overcoming Common Problems Series

How to Cope with Stress
DR PETER TYRER

How to Cope with your Child's Allergies
DR PAUL CARSON

How to Cope with your Nerves
DR TONY LAKE

How to Cope with Tinnitus and Hearing Loss
DR ROBERT YOUNGSON

How to Do What You Want to Do
DR PAUL HAUCK

How to Enjoy Your Old Age
DR B. F. SKINNER AND M. E.
VAUGHAN

How to Interview and Be Interviewed
MICHELE BROWN AND
GYLES BRANDRETH

How to Improve Your Confidence
DR KENNETH HAMBLY

How to Love a Difficult Man
NANCY GOOD

How to Love and be Loved
DR PAUL HAUCK

How to Make Successful Decisions
ALISON HARDINGHAM

How to Pass Your Driving Test
DONALD RIDLAND

How to Say No to Alcohol
KEITH McNEILL

How to Sleep Better
DR PETER TYRER

How to Stand up for Yourself
DR PAUL HAUCK

How to Start a Conversation and Make
Friends
DON GABOR

How to Stop Feeling Guilty
DR VERNON COLEMAN

How to Stop Smoking
GEORGE TARGET

How to Stop Taking Tranquillisers
DR PETER TYRER

If Your Child is Diabetic
JOANNE ELLIOTT

Jealousy
DR PAUL HAUCK

Learning to Live with Multiple Sclerosis
DR ROBERT POVEY, ROBIN DOWIE
AND GILLIAN PRETT

Living with Grief
DR TONY LAKE

Living Through Personal Crisis
ANN KAISER STEARNS

Living with High Blood Pressure
DR TOM SMITH

Loneliness
DR TONY LAKE

Making Marriage Work
DR PAUL HAUCK

Making the Most of Loving
GILL COX AND SHEILA DAINOW

Making the Most of Yourself
GILL COX AND SHEILA DAINOW

Making Relationships Work
CHRISTINE SANDFORD AND WYN
BEARDSLEY

Meeting People is Fun
How to overcome shyness
DR PHYLLIS SHAW

Nervous Person's Companion
DR KENNETH HAMBLY

One Parent Families
DIANA DAVENPORT

Overcoming Fears and Phobias
DR TONY WHITEHEAD

Overcoming Stress
DR VERNON COLEMAN

Overcoming Tension
DR KENNETH HAMBLY

Overcoming Common Problems Series

Contents

Acknowledgements

My interest in the treatment of mood swings was aroused by Dr Joseph Meehan who, as Medical Director of St Patrick's Hospital, Dublin, gave me the necessary encouragement and support to embark on this project. I owe him an immense debt.

Professors Norman Moore and Karl O'Sullivan, Mrs Gillian Corcoran and Mr Michael Connolly made useful comments on the various drafts and I thank them for their help.

Finally, I express my sincere appreciation to the many patients and relatives, without whom this book would never have been written, and who taught me so much about the personal aspects of mood swings.

Foreword

Disorders of mood account for by far the greatest demand for psychiatric consultations. An increasing public awareness of their diverse nature coupled with a lessening tendency to conceal psychological symptoms has resulted in more sufferers from depression and elation seeking medical help.

Similar trends have been noticed in the United States of America. Since the publication there in the past few years of the third edition of the *Diagnostic and Statistical Manual of Mental Disorders*, known to Psychiatrists as DSM–111, the clinical features of conditions associated with disturbances of mood have been more clearly delineated. As a result, some illnesses formerly classified among the neuroses or the schizophrenias are now recognised as springing from disorders of mental disposition or mood.

It is timely, therefore, that a clinician such as Dr McKeon, with experience and skill in handling the management of these conditions, should outline his views and observations in book form. It is certain that both the sufferers and their families will be enlightened by its contents and be reassured by the knowledge that nowadays one can combine not only strategies of treatment involving medical, social and psychological techniques, but successful preventive measures as well.

P. J. Meehan MB, FRCPI, FRC, PSYCH, DPM

Introduction

This story is about people, people we all know. We meet them in the street, buy our newspaper from them, they preach to us on Sundays and care for us when we are sick, they design our homes and govern our country. They are people like you and me, with real feelings and aspirations. Their mood swings set them apart; for some these are mild and innocuous, for others they are grossly incapacitating and are referred to as manic-depressive moods.

Depression and elation are probably the oldest recorded mental illnesses and have been described in the Old Testament and in the works of Homer and Hippocrates. Over the centuries, from the pens of educated sufferers came accounts of inexplicable moods ranging from utter despair to periods of prolonged joy or ecstasy. The few who recognised their distress as an illness seem to have accepted it as part of the human condition while others went unrecognised or misdiagnosed.

Although graphic descriptions of individual mood swings have existed from the earliest days of civilisation, the association between the opposite extremes of mood was not widely accepted by doctors until the nineteenth century. In 1854, Jean Falret, a French psychiatrist, published a description of cyclical mental illness, calling it *la folie circulaire*. Throughout Europe at that time other psychiatrists were reporting similar observations. The eminent German psychiatrist, Emil Kraepelin, impressed by these studies, proposed the name 'manic-depressive illness' in 1896 to characterise recurrent episodes of depression and elation and went on to propose a classification to distinguish mood disorders from other mental illnesses. This classification has been the cornerstone of twentieth-century psychiatry, and his astute observations have been confirmed by present-day researchers who now recognise three patterns of mood swings: recurrent depression; recurrent depression alternating with bouts of elation; and recurrent elation.

Once mood disorders were characterised as a distinct illness, the quest for a cure started in earnest. In the early decades of the twentieth century the dramatic advances in medicine and the

1

interest aroused by the Freudian view of emotional disturbances created an optimistic outlook for disorders of the mind. Expectations of major therapeutic advances, however, went unfulfilled and had to take their place behind the slow march of history. Treatments such as hydrotherapy and non-specific sedatives were all that were available and sufferers had to wait patiently for a spontaneous break in the illness.

Dramatic breakthroughs occurred in the 1950s with the discovery of anti-depressant pills and a range of treatments for controlling elation or mania. For the first time individual episodes of depression and elation could be successfully treated, thus lessening the train of human suffering. However, these drugs did little to prevent the pattern of recurrent mood swings. Lithium was to change all that. Although first used to treat elation in 1949, it took many years of intensive research before its value as a preventive of mood swings was recognised. Today it is the principal treatment for recurrent manic depression and has proved to be a safe and effective medication. This discovery has radically altered the outlook for patients all over the world and has made their wish for a normal life a reality.

Unfortunately, achieving stability is often hampered by a variety of difficulties. First among these is the failure to recognise that a mood swing is occurring. Even today a person in the midst of a mood change may be as beguiled by the experience as a fellow sufferer of centuries ago. Depression may be mistaken for fatigue or anaemia, or masquerade as insomnia or one of a legion of bodily complaints. Elation is even more deceptive; its boundless energy, and grandiose and witty manner may be what the patient is most aware of, but others, particularly family members, will know the impatience, impaired judgement and many indiscretions. Inevitably, unrecognised depressions and elations will leave their mark on many facets of the patient's life. So spotting a mood change in its early stages becomes the first step to successful treatment.

'Manic depression' is still considered a horrifying term and conjures up images of violence, unpredictability and sheer madness. Sufferers from the illness recoil when they first hear the diagnosis and their deep sense of dread often prevents them both learning about the illness and coming to terms with its reality, which ultimately leads to a rejection of treatment. Many a

2

traveller along the path of acceptance has faltered in the face of his doubts or was waylaid by well-meaning friends who assailed him on the evils of his 'drug' taking. Most are keen to know the facts and be advised about preventive measures.

A mood swing is not a private affair. By its nature it not only affects every aspect of the sufferer's emotional life but also his relatives and friends. They may be unsure of what is happening, have difficulty recognising the moods, blame themselves or others, and may despair of ever having the illness remedied. How they cope with these difficulties and adapt to the changing moods will have immense influence on the final outcome. Their understanding, support and guidance is as crucial as any other aspect of the treatment.

Four years ago I was approached by some relatives of patients with mood swings who felt little was being done to help them cope with the emotional burden imposed by the illness. They were bewildered, felt alone in their plight and many had never heard terms such as elation, mood swings and manic-depressive illness. We agreed to meet weekly to discuss their difficulties without any other aim in mind. From the start this gathering of relatives began to see that they had much in common. They described the dread of elation, how depressions were much more manageable and, seeing the similarities in each other's accounts, they found support and realised that they could make sense of what had often previously been a chaotic situation. They learned to recognise a mood change in its early stages, became more supportive and encouraging, and helped the patient to limit the effect of the mood swings. It soon became obvious that the patients were just as much in need of a factual understanding of their illness and its implications if they were to achieve a durable stability. From this evolved a regular series of group meetings and lectures for patients and relatives where they could share and learn from each other, and grasp the facts about the illness. I have been encouraged by the many patients and relatives who have benefited from a realistic understanding of the illness and its treatment to give some direction to those who follow in their footsteps. This book is a summary of the contents of the discussions and lectures.

Throughout the book's seven chapters the emphasis is on the practical aspects of coping with the illness. You will learn what is meant by elation and depression, how to detect them in their early stages, and how to recognise the different types of mood swing. Descriptions of the complications that may arise and how they can be prevented are accompanied by some case histories. Next, the focus is on the causes of mood swings, and the effects of stress, childhood experiences, heredity and seasonal factors are considered. Here you will see how a variety of factors interact to produce mood swings and get some indication of why a treatment such as lithium works. The treatment of elation and depression is distinguished from their prevention, and the role of anti-depressant tablets, ECT, lithium, and psychotherapy is covered in detail. You will find practical and constructive advice on how to spot and limit the effects of mood swings. Throughout, much emphasis is given to the important role of the family. The final chapter answers a range of questions frequently posed by patients and relatives.

Finally, throughout this book the patient is referred to as 'he'. This is by no means to imply that all sufferers of depression are male, and 'he or she' is to be understood throughout.

1

Recognising Mood Swings

'If they only understood what happens to me. I know they are hurt by all of this but if only they could understand how I feel. If it was a broken leg or something it would be different—at least they would see it.' The sense of frustration is just as strong on the other side of the emotional wall: 'Why does she go on like this? I get down at times too, but I have to keep going—I just cannot understand it. If only she had the will-power.' Such are the exasperated feelings of a patient and her relative trying in vain to break the mould of misunderstanding. Neither will succeed unless they first recognise that manic depression is an illness like any other, with features which set it apart both from normal feelings of sadness and high spirits and from other types of depression.

Depression: from sadness to illness

Given the everyday experience of depression, how does one recognise a depressive illness? Dips in mood are very much a familiar and commonplace experience occurring usually in response to adverse circumstances which can be anything from the seemingly trivial matter of getting a parking ticket to an obviously upsetting event such as the death of a close relative. Daily friendships, kind words or exceptionally good news, and most importantly our ability to look on the bright side of things, tend to lessen the hurt. The result is that for most of us life has its ups and downs but they are mild and short-lived.

Depression is a very normal experience. We have all felt it at some time or other and it is usually there for a very good reason. A death in the family naturally evokes feelings of sadness and loneliness with tearful spells. This is the way the mind reacts when we lose somebody or something in which we have invested our emotions. At other times what is lost is not very clear. In a sense we feel the loss but cannot say why we feel sad. This can happen, for example, when we take a particular friendship for granted. Then when it ends the feeling part of our brain feels hurt but the knowing or intellectual side is as yet unable to tell us why we are upset. This often happens when the loss is of something less tangible; a hope or a plan gone wrong or an ambition that is never going to be realised. These losses are all very real in the mind's eye and in such instances we should not dismiss our feelings but rather ask what has gone wrong. Appropriate feelings of sadness seem to serve some purpose, just as does pain which is the body's signal to slow down and take corrective action. Sadness is the mind's way of making us stop and take stock of what has gone wrong and this is the first step in coming to terms with our loss.

Another type of normal depression is the variation in mood that occurs with the changing seasons. Many people find that during the winter months they have less energy, that they seem to need more sleep and are inclined to doze easily. For some, this seasonal variation in activity is accompanied by feelings of sadness, a less optimistic outlook, and a tendency to be less sociable. Spring then brings an upsurge in energy and enthusiasm and an increased level of activity which persists until autumn. It is unlikely that the seasonal variations in temperature can fully explain these mood shifts.

Such mild and almost imperceptible mood changes are normal. What then is an abnormal mood? Sadness or feelings of depression which are particularly long-lasting or severe are called abnormal depressions. This means that the dividing line betwen normal and abnormal depression is one of degree, just as is the difference between normal body temperature and fever. How is this dividing line defined? Doctors can grade the severity of depression by referring to the degree of sadness the person is experiencing, whether his sleep or appetite is affected, and how much his self-esteem and outlook on life have changed. In practice, however, it is when the person who is depressed decides that he needs help that the diagnosis of an abnormal depression is made. So while in theory deciding between a normal and abnormal depression might prove difficult, in reality it is not a problem.

The different types of depression

Generations of doctors and researchers have attempted to define the different types of depression on the basis of their symptoms and signs, possible causes and a host of biochemical and hereditary factors. Their limited success is due more to the complexity of the

6

human mind than to any lack of enthusiasm or endeavour on their part. Despite this imperfect state of affairs we do have a classification of depression based on the clinical features which has a widely accepted usefulness in deciding what treatment is likely to be effective. Four main types of depression can be identified.

1. *Reactive depression*

This is the commonest type of depression and is simply an extension of the normal upset feelings following a loss of some kind. When upset feelings become more severe or prolonged— such that the individual finds them to be more than he is used to or able to cope with—he becomes depressed.

Typically a person with reactive depression will feel low, anxious, often angry and irritable, tends to be at a low ebb in the evenings and has difficulty getting off to sleep. His mind is preoccupied with thoughts that just will not go away, he often overeats and tends to find refuge in sleep. Usually this type of depression is not particularly severe in that the person will often get relief in talking with friends or by going out for an evening. This is not to say that it is not a distressing experience for the person concerned. Indeed, many are preoccupied with suicidal thoughts and some resort to overdoses of tablets or other self-destructive acts. Peter describes how he felt when he knew his relationship with Sarah was ending:

At first I just felt numb, almost unreal, and I was in a world of my own. When I could feel, it was a mixture of sadness and anger—angry with her, angry with myself for being such a fool—and I didn't know what to do. I became more and more anxious especially when I got pains in my chest. At night I had dreams of attacking people, over and over again.

Peter and Sarah had been dating one another for three years and hoped to marry in a year or so. They decided not to finalise their marriage plans until they had enough money to buy a house. Their savings were progressing well until Sarah decided to go abroad for a month's holiday with a girlfriend. Although Peter knew this would set their wedding back by at least a year he did not dissent. However, when she was gone he became depressed and felt no better on Sarah's return. Gradually he began to realise that they

7

were drifting apart and had to accept that the expensive holiday was just one more sign of Sarah's unspoken reluctance to proceed with the wedding. When he was able to discuss his feelings and their implications he realised why he felt so low. In time he spoke with Sarah, expressed his annoyance and disappointment and was then gradually able to come to terms with what had happened and end their relationship.

2. Neurotic depression

At one end of the vulnerability spectrum is the well-adjusted individual who will only experience a reactive depression when faced with exceptional loss or profound emotional trauma, and at the other end is the person with an unstable personality who finds minor misfortunes intolerable. Those who get recurrent episodes of reactive depression will often be found to have personality difficulties which both hamper their ability to deal with life's problems and cope with the emotional impact of these problems. Such mood changes are referred to as neurotic depressions.

There are many personality types which are prone to depression but two in particular are worth mentioning. One is the obsessional perfectionist who has a very precise and rigid approach to life. Such personalities demand a lot of themselves and others and while they may meet their own targets they will frequently be disappointed by others. When trains fail to run on time, when people are late for appointments or children wear muddy shoes across their highly polished floor their annoyance and disappointment can easily turn to depression. If the obsessional person is not able to meet his own high expectations he will feel guilty and morose.

The other personality type that is predisposed to depression is the excessively passive individual who persistently avoids asserting himself. He dreads conflict, and, wanting to please everybody, finds it hard to say 'no' and ends up by being hurt. He hides his injured feelings and over the years an accumulation of the hurts seeps out as depression, anxiety or panic attacks. Here is a typical story. Deirdre had been married for three years when her first baby was born and she decided to stop working to look after her child. All was going well until she began to feel depressed. Her husband said that she had been very moody and tearful of late, tended to pick arguments and that he found her impossible to

8

please. Deirdre confirmed this account and added that she was very shaky and panicky, particularly when she met her neighbours. She had agreed to look after three other toddlers for neighbouring women who went out to work but, although she felt very annoyed with her neighbours for imposing, and berated herself for tacitly accepting their requests, she had never mentioned how she felt other than to her husband. He wanted to discuss the problem with their neighbours but she would not allow him do so, lest they be offended. She eventually saw that her depressive symptoms and anxiety were the result of hidden and unexpressed anger which at times was misdirected at her husband. She had had previous depressions, which were likewise traced to bottled-up emotions and Deirdre soon began to realise that her reluctance to be assertive in her dealings with other people was the basis of her mood changes. When, with encouragement, she spoke to her neighbours and told them she would be no longer able to look after their children she felt immediate relief. Since then she has gone on to tackle other troubled relationships with confidence.

3. Endogenous depression

Endogenous depression means depression coming from within. In its pure form the sufferer is unable to account for his mood change as it hits him out of the blue, he is impervious to good news and is generally more distraught than the sufferer of reactive depression. Distinguishing features include a sense of hopelessness and despair, self-doubt and low self-esteem, waking early in the morning, poor appetite, weight loss and an all-pervading indifference to former concerns. The person's thinking slows, he has difficulty in concentrating and making decisions, and everything seems an effort. Frank describes his depression occurring after business problems:

I found my partner was cheating on me—he had been planning to start up in business on his own by taking away some of our agencies. I just couldn't believe it—we had built up the company over the years and worked very well together. We eventually came to a satisfactory financial arrangement and in that sense his parting worked out very well. Somehow I just slumped into a depression. I didn't want to talk to anybody, I

COPING WITH DEPRESSION AND ELATION

felt empty, couldn't think straight and just stared into space. My wife said I was like a zombie and I hadn't washed or shaved for weeks.

Frank rarely smiled, was sleeping poorly and had lost a stone in weight in a few weeks. His depression responded to a course of anti-depressant medication and he was able to take control of his life again. While he could point to his business problems as the reason for his depression, many others with similar signs and symptoms cannot identify any precipitant. As we will see later, anti-depressant tablets are the main treatment for this type of depression but due attention should also be given, on recovery, to any upsetting event which may have brought on the mood change.

Endogenous depression is mainly of biological origin and tends to run in families. Nevertheless, those who have inherited a tendency towards this form of depression may never become depressed unless they are exposed to some stressful event.

4. The depression characteristic of manic depression

Signs and symptoms of this form of depression are indistinguishable from those of the endogenous variety except for the unique spells of elation with which it alternates. Because of the distress people are subjected to, with few exceptions they readily recognise this depression as an illness, while the elation, by contrast, is more elusive and is considered an illness only in its more pronounced form. After briefly digressing to look at secondary depression, we will return to a description of the features of both mood phases.

Secondary depression

This refers to mood changes secondary to other medical and psychiatric illness. The most familiar is probably a depression following a bout of flu. Depression also occurs with many other viral infections, anaemias, vitamin deficiencies, thyroid and other glandular disorders. Certain treatments such as steroids and blood pressure tablets can also induce mood changes. Of the psychological disorders, schizophrenia is frequently accompanied by depression and often requires to be actively treated in its own right. Alcohol is probably the most commonly used mood-altering drug and, in large quantities, both causes depression and makes any form of depression worse.

Mood swings

A mood swing refers to the mood changes of endogenous depression and manic depressive illness ('manic depression'). We have already seen that these two types of depression are outwardly very similar. Mood fluctuations in both cases tend to be relatively autonomous in the sense that they usually occur in the absence of an obvious stress and have a biological basis. In fact these two types of mood swings have a great deal in common and for all practical purposes the only difference worth mentioning is that manic depression alternates with bouts of elation while endogenous depression does not.

Manic depression. Signs and symptoms of the depressive phase

Early symptoms of this depression include undue tiredness, slowed thinking with poor concentration, loss of enthusiasm progressing to apathy, and a sense of despair. Indecision is the rule and gloomy thoughts of the past dominate. Time seems interminably long and retreat from the hustle and bustle of life seems to bring relief. Conversation is replaced by lengthy silences and thinking can demand an enormous effort. Michael, a 46-year-old experienced and successful computer salesman describes how his depression began:

I just felt run down and found it hard to drum up new business. My wife suggested we take a holiday—it was absolute agony. I became more withdrawn, stared into space and just wanted to be in bed all day. I felt so tired and everything was an effort—simply deciding what to wear took an age.

I thought I was coming down with a virus so we cut our holiday short and went to see our family doctor. He said I was run down, took a blood test and prescribed vitamins. As the weeks went by there was no improvement and my boss began to comment on my poor sales performance. He had noticed that I was avoiding clients and he gave me the usual Dale Carnegie pep talk. It was no good, I just could not sell. After that I spent most of my time in bed staring at the ceiling. I had no interest in anything, including food—only alcohol gave me a kick and helped me sleep. When I look back on the agony of those three months I think of how near I came to killing myself.

Such are the words of a man surrounded by the forces of depression—bewildered and subdued, lingering on the brink of suicide and yet unaware of the nature of the problem— depression.

Loss of interest touches almost every aspect of the sufferer's life; food seems tasteless, work becomes boring and feelings for those closest wane. Initiative is dampened, leading to poor performance at work and this is particularly telling in those who are dependent on their creativity or, as in Michael's case, drive for their living. Their spontaneous reactions, which are dependent on effective concentration, dwindle, often resulting in serious accidents; the cooker grill which accidentally catches fire, a hammer being dropped from scaffolding on a building site or a car being driven heedlessly through a red light are some of the less obvious hazards of depression.

One patient, Catherine, an attractive 34-year-old housewife, knew what was happening from the start:

I had seen my father get depressed like this — he had been attending psychiatrists since we were babies. I became cranky and tired but still slept fitfully. Thinking back on my first depression, the thing that surprises me most was that I felt my husband didn't love me—I just felt unwanted—not that I could really say why—and I had lost all interest in sex. When the depression was treated my feelings returned and I saw how foolish I had been. We were always very close—it just wasn't me.

Uncharacteristic tiredness often leads to napping during the day and usually the person has little difficulty in getting to sleep at night. Their night's sleep is typically interrupted by frequent wakenings and they are often unable to get back to sleep after 5 a.m. At the outset, the feeling of gloom and despair is worse in the early morning and lessens as the day progresses; later in the illness there is no evening respite.

A depressive mood swing can vary from mild tiredness and lessening of zest without a strong feeling of depression, to a state where the sufferer is withdrawn, mute, bedridden and neglects to feed himself. Typically this trough in mood occurs 'out of the blue' and only rarely can one attribute the symptoms to an upsetting incident. A gradual onset is usual but in some instances the depression starts more dramatically. For one patient, an experienced nurse, the first signs came so precipitously that her family, seeing her age overnight, thought she had a stroke. She described waking in the morning feeling bemused, wandering aimlessly and being overcome with despair.

Masked depression

So far I have dealt with what one might call obvious depression; the patient complains of feeling depressed and the doctor confirms this diagnosis. However, depression is not always that conspicuous. Masked depression is the term used to refer to a variety of different expressions of depressive illnesses where the patient typically does not feel depressed but complains of some other psychological or physical symptom. This happens most often in depressive mood swings *but can be seen in any form of depression*. Let us now look at the three different types of masked depression.

The first type to consider are those who experience many of the symptoms usually associated with a depressive illness such as extreme tiredness or insomnia but who do not actually feel depressed. As far as they are concerned they may simply feel tired. Michael's symptoms started in just this manner: he complained of feeling run down. He never used the word depression to describe how he felt and was surprised when told the diagnosis.

In the second type of masked depression the usual symptoms of depression are either not present or are hidden behind more prominent psychological or physical symptoms not commonly associated with depression. Here, it would appear that the hidden depression has released other symptoms which then dominate the clinical picture. In such instances the person may feel mainly anxious, panicky, or may experience any of a number of psychological or bodily symptoms: thus depression can masquerade as an anxiety, phobic or obsessive neurosis, a schizophrenia-like illness or as any of the wide variety of bodily symptoms of hypochondriasis. While at first sight the person may be complaining of

13

what appears to be anything from a simple anxiety state to angina, on closer scrutiny the despondency, poor concentration and insomnia characteristic of depression will be found. Two brief case histories will help to illustrate the point. Joan describes the onset of her symptoms following the birth of her child as follows:

> At first I started to worry about little things; was the baby getting enough milk, was the house tidy, why was my husband late home from work—did he have an accident. It went on and on like that. I felt extremely anxious and just couldn't relax— even with yoga. I sweated a lot and my throat was sore all the time—I thought I might have cancer. To cut a long story short—after seeing various throat specialists who assured me that there was nothing wrong with my throat, my GP eventually convinced me to take anti-depressant tablets—I was better in a matter of weeks. I never thought I was depressed.

Another patient describes how he felt convinced that people at work were spying on him and were watching his every move. Some stock was missing and he felt that people were accusing him of its theft. In a bizarre way he thought they were probably right and he really was quite evil. He was unable to confide in any of his friends or family and gradually became more withdrawn. When he was brought to his family doctor he simply requested that the doctor help put a stop to the persecution at work. Behind the façade of paranoid delusions were symptoms of apathy, poor concentration, weight loss and insomnia—all pointing to a severe depression.

Those who traipse from doctor to doctor with a multitude of physical symptoms often have the most inconspicuous depression. Despite their repeated visits to specialists with symptoms such as pains in the legs, burning sensation when passing urine, or discoloration of the tongue they are not convinced when told that there is nothing wrong. Even their relatives tell them it is their imagination. Eventually, and as a last resort, they are referred to a psychiatrist. Relief from these disabling symptoms with anti-depressants or psychotherapy is often quite dramatic.

The final type of masked depression is where the mood change, for a variety of reasons, has gone unrecognised and the patient comes forward with a complication of depression such as alcoholism, a marital problem or poor work performance. Increasing dependence on alcohol or sleeping tablets is often an early sign of depression. If the person becomes addicted to these drugs the symptoms of depression may not be obvious. Much of our everyday activity which does not need conscious thought is, however, dependent on effective concentration, and so is vulnerable during depression. This is how a mood change can, by impairing the mind's ability to concentrate, lead to accidents in the home, at work and on the road. Marital friction can, on occasions, be the only manifestation of a depression in one or other partner. Here, his loss of interest affects that which is most important to him—his marriage. The person may feel unloved and unwanted without actually realising that it is his inability to feel these emotions that is the problem.

These diverse manifestations of depression often result in delayed diagnosis and needless misery. They emphasise the fact that one does not have to feel depressed to be depressed.

Elation: from high spirits to illness

Ordinary good spirits, like sadness, are part of everyday living; they reflect how life is treating us. When we feel in control of our world, can see ourselves in a favourable light, and have the respect of those who matter we are usually happy. But there is happiness and elation, and the mind is not as discriminating in distinguishing these as it is when separating sadness from depression—being happy, in a sense, it sees no point in the exercise. With normal feelings of high spirits the person's judgement is balanced, they have control over their mood and more importantly, day-to-day reverses will dampen their mood appropriately. Persistent and inappropriate high spirits which are not in keeping with the person's usual personality are called elation or mania.

Mania: signs and symptoms

Elation or mania, the opposite of depression, although usually pleasurable, often has a more devastating effect on a person's life. What makes it particularly serious is that the afflicted individual is usually at first quite unaware of his abnormal mood and simply feels uncharacteristically zestful and enthusiastic. Accompanying this euphoric state, the person finds their thoughts speeded up or racing. Rapid thinking in turn leads to quick talking and hurried activity. Speeding recklessly while driving, walking with a sense of urgency and, all in all, racing against the clock, are characteristic of elation. And it is very hard to switch off the hyperactive mind at bedtime—the person will toss and turn, his head buzzing with ideas.

By contrast with the depressed phase, where the person's thinking is generally self-deprecatory and concerned with the past, the elated person directs his attention to the future with grandiose and daring ideas. Initially, these plans may be realistic but as the person's judgement becomes increasingly blinded by its own optimism the mindless follies are obvious to all. Just as the person's mind jumps from one idea to another so too they flit from one incompleted venture to another.

Michael describes how, after months of depression, his mood began to change:

The ball and chain which had been holding me down seemed lighter. I had been under great pressure at work as my sales average was dismal and with five months left in my sales year it seemed unlikely that I would make the yearly minimum required by our firm.

In August things began to pick up — I was able to rise in the morning without feeling like a ton of lead. I felt alive again and everyone told me how well I looked. Sales just fell into my lap. At first I thought I was picking up business which had accumulated during the months of depression. Life seemed so sweet, everything was going my way. Over those heady months between August and December I achieved so many sales I was made salesman of the year and I came top of the class in a sales technique course which I had been avoiding for years.

Looking back on this high which in many ways seemed perfect, I must say that I felt tense—as if my body could not keep up with my racing mind. I would lie awake at night thinking of all I was going to do the following day and would be as bright as a lark after four hours' sleep, much to my wife's annoyance. People in the office were amazed at my energy. I was in great spirits, so much so that while having Christmas drinks with colleagues, a newcomer to the firm jokingly said that I had too much to drink, not realising that I never take alcohol. I was very embarrassed and began to realise that something was wrong. Another thing—I tended to be argumentative—a neighbour's shrubs had been shading the sunlight from my roses for years but I never mentioned it until I was elated and in the end we had a flaming row.

Religion, art, music and literature seem revitalised, there is a new appreciation of friends, and what formerly held a certain attraction now poses an irresistible urge. Increased sexual desire often leads to impulsive sexual relationships and uncharacteristic extra-marital affairs. Ill-considered spending on expensive and unwanted items or worthless trinkets is all too frequent an occurrence. As one elated patient aptly put it, 'all that glitters seems like gold'.

Martin, a prosperous industrialist, had been admitted to hospital after an overdose of sleeping tablets. Over the years he had been having spells of depression and had become dependent on alcohol. In the course of our conversation I learnt that he had spent the weeks prior to this depression flying between the European capitals and had negotiated a multi-million pound meat export order without any idea where he might get the meat. Hearing a rumour that an airport was to be sited near his home town, he purchased a large tract of land which he hoped to resell to the developers. Martin tells what he was like when he came home:

I felt like a wound-up coil unfolding—everything seemed possible and within my grasp. What I achieved during the high was minute when compared with my unfulfilled schemes. When I came back from Europe I felt caged in at home; my stage seemed to have shrunk and I was fighting with everybody.

All in all, the manic patient is apt to report that he never felt so well. To the objective onlooker at home, and to a lesser extent at work, the story is quite different . They too can see the pleasurable side of the mood change with its heightened spirits and charming and engaging personality, but having more of a foothold in reality they are painfully aware of the devastating effect of the illness. Family members who have to rise in the early hours of the morning to participate in the elated person's schemes, employers who are besieged with directions on how to run their businesses,

17

employees who are expected to have tomorrow's work done yesterday and husbands or wives who see large overdrafts accumulate through reckless spending or who hear of their partner's extra-marital affairs recounted in an unabashed manner, will all attest to the havoc of elation. The most the elated person can be aware of at this stage will be their racing thoughts and difficulty in sleeping for more than a few hours. Their new found energy and charisma means little to their family and close friends who are swept aside by the manic wave—such are the two faces of elation.

Depressive mood swings are invariably described as distressful or painful for the person concerned; that is not so with elation. For Michael and Martin, the early stage of their elation went totally unnoticed. In its milder forms elation goes unrecognised by all but the most experienced observer, and at its most severe it is often only diagnosed following a catastrophe.

Philosophers, poets, novelists and biographers have throughout the ages recounted their personal experiences of moods in graphic terms. Among the accomplished personalities of the twentieth century can be found several eminent people who had well-defined periods of elation and depression. People such as Ernest Hemingway, Virginia Woolf, Dylan Thomas, Vivien Leigh, Brendan Behan, Theodore Roosevelt, Winston Churchill and Mao Tse-tung knew what it was to be without hope and then to feel the rushing torrents of exhilaration. Some had the breadth of personality or the scope of high office to harness their moods successfully, while others succumbed to their uncontrollable emotions.

Elation, in its early stages, is often creative and fruitful; it gives the person a new awareness and fills him with the courage and determination to step outside his usual sphere, often allowing him to accomplish amazing feats. Some who have experienced this will say that a person has not really lived until they have experienced elation and they are reluctant to give up their highs. Others are wiser; they know too well that sooner or later depression will follow almost as often as night follows day, and can see the stark reality of the other side of elation.

Not all phases of elation are pleasant. Most people in this mood have moments of distressing agitation and anger, or will feel an intense pressure in their head and body which they describe as the

18

frustration of not been able to get things done in an instant. They sometimes come to dread the nightly battle with their racing mind when trying to get to sleep. All of these unpleasant symptoms occur when the speeding thoughts are more than mind or body can take. For most, however, these experiences are fleeting and soon forgotten about when the sense of well being and zest return and the racing thoughts lessen.

The occasional patient with elation will describe his mood swing as being distressing throughout. The incessant whirlwind of thought jars against his mind and he feels as if his head is about to explode. His heightened activity, which he describes as extreme restlessness, is also unpleasant. Talking brings him relief. Again, the most likely explanation for this distressing mood is that the racing thoughts have outstripped the brain's ability to assimilate and process them. Eileen's 'elations' have always been like this. In fact she thought they were depressions, as they were so unpleasant:

I felt angry with everyone and was always about to explode. Nothing seemed right. My whole body was in a knot and I just couldn't switch off. I talked and talked and, I'm sure, nearly drove everyone mad.

As you would expect, Eileen quickly sought treatment and was thus spared many of the problems to which those with the more usual form of elation are prone.

Mood swing patterns

The time from the beginning of one mood swing to the start of another is called a cycle (see Figure 1 on p. 20). This cycle may consist of a phase of elation followed by a short period of normal mood lasting a few hours to two weeks, then a downswing to depression and, finally, a return to normal mood. An untreated elation lasts anything from days or weeks to months and the subsequent depression may be longer. Modern-day treatment has dramatically curtailed the frequency and intensity of these cycles.

If a person has had just one episode of elation and depression, he is not necessarily going to have continuing mood swings. In fact various surveys have shown that 30 to 50 per cent of those with one

1983	1984	1985	1986

MONTHS OF THE YEAR

JFMAMJJASOND   JFMAMJJASOND   JFMAMJJASOND   JFMAMJJASOND

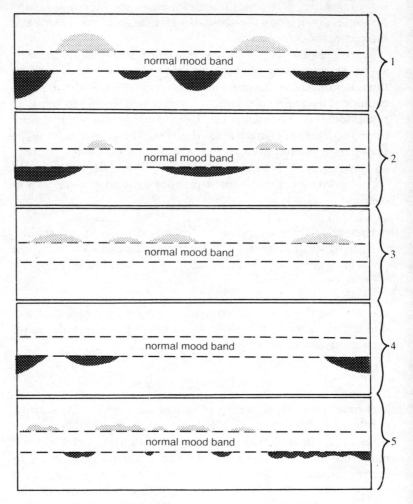

Figure 1: DIFFERENT PATTERNS OF UNTREATED MOOD SWINGS.
1 Severe depressions followed by equally intense elations.
2 Severe depressions with mild elations.
3 Recurrent elation.
4 Recurrent depression.
5 Short and relatively milder mood swings.

Elation

Depression

20

episode will not have a recurrence. However, for those who have had three or more separate mood swing cycles the chance of further episodes, if untreated, are very high. Fortunately, effective preventative treatment is available for those with such an established pattern (see Chapter 4).

While the symptoms which dominate an individual mood swing may vary from one person to the next, the difference is one of emphasis — the symptoms described above are what the moods have in common. But there are real differences between patients: Michael's elation was followed by depression, whereas for Catherine, the depression came first, and Martin's elation was more intense than Michael's. If you refer to Figure 1 you will see how mood swings can be subclassified into different types on the basis of the frequency, intensity and sequence of the moods.

Identifying the particular mood swing type has a certain usefulness; for the patient with an established pattern of mood swings it is possible to predict with some accuracy what pattern of mood changes they might expect, and for the doctor it helps in the selection of the appropriate treatment.

2
What Can Go Wrong?

You might rightly ask what else can go wrong. We have seen how abnormal moods pose a tremendous problem for an individual's judgement and discretion. His thoughts are subtly influenced to a greater or lesser extent by the mood change. The well-adjusted person with a relatively mild mood swing will often realise that his thinking has changed and hold it in check. Others are not so fortunate; through either lack of insight or the intensity of the mood swing the distorted thinking dominates and dictates uncharacteristic behaviour. Such are the complications of manic-depressive illness.

Alcohol and drug dependence

Those with mood swings are particularly prone to rely on alcohol and tranquillising drugs. Doctors know from experience that increasing reliance on drink and sleeping tablets is often an early indicator of depression.

The depressed person will tend to find that alcohol numbs his painful thoughts, and it is often the only way he can ensure a good night's sleep. Next morning the depression is just as intense and for many it is considerably worse. Some continue to drink to excess for this short-lived relief while others, realising that alcohol is not the answer, reduce their intake. Likewise in elation, alcohol is often used as a prop. Being a readily available sedative, it is widely used to slow the racing mind and help with sleep.

Not infrequently, those diagnosed as alcoholics have an underlying mood disorder which is not always immediately obvious. It can be impossible to detect the symptoms of a true depression beneath the feelings of despondency, early-morning gloom and sleep disturbance of alcohol dependence, or distinguish the uncharacteristic behaviour of elation from the exuberance of intoxication. Often when the person has managed to stop drinking for a few weeks the full range of their mood swings is exposed. Paul's story is typical of many patients who are first treated for a drink problem:

I had been drinking heavily for about three months and I just couldn't stop. The mornings were the worst—I would waken after a few hours sleep, shaking all over, and had to have a drink. I was very restless and, for some reason, angry with the world. After much persuasion I saw my doctor who advised me to stop drinking and gave me tablets to help me get over the withdrawal. Initially I felt great, but as the weeks went by I became more and more restless, couldn't get to sleep and my brain just wouldn't switch off.

Paul's wife described his grandiose plans, overtalkativeness and incessant activity—all characteristic signs of elation.

A similar trend is becoming apparent among those who use drugs such as narcotics, amphetamines and LSD. From time to time patients are brought along by their relatives requesting that they be treated for their drug problem, when the main reason for their wayward and unusual behaviour is a hidden mood disorder. Those prone to mood swings or any other psychological disorder are more likely to rely on drugs to cope with their distress, and almost always they are unaware of what the real problem is.

Overspending and underspending

Whether we are pleased or displeased with an event often says more about our mood at the time than the event itself. Just as mood colours our perception so does it influence the decisions which follow. Let us look at a typical decision and see how a mood swing can affect judgement. When we are considering buying a new car, for example, our thoughts go something like this: I would really like that car—it looks good, it's easy on fuel and it's very comfortable—but it's rather expensive—maybe I should wait until I buy the new furniture we need—then again the salesman says that there will be a price increase next month—maybe it would cost less in that garage across town—and so on. Thus the decision is carefully considered and whether we buy or not depends on the fine balance between the positive and negative aspects of the potential purchase.

In depression, the person will tend to see more of the negative features and, as such, will be unduly thrifty. While this is usually harmless, in a more severe depression the person's judgement may be so impaired that they refuse to buy food and clothing sufficient for survival. They will tend to underestimate their self-worth and abilities, undervalue their property and other assets and often be convinced of their impoverished state. Because of these misperceptions, the depressed person may try to make amends for imagined guilty deeds or minor indiscretions from their past, refuse to collect social welfare benefits believing that they are undeserving, or sell property and other goods below their market value. One such person going through a prolonged depression felt she had not been able to do a full day's work at the bank and concluded, because of this, that she was cheating her employer and made amends by not cashing her pay cheques.

In elation, by contrast, the positive aspects of the purchase dominate, and reckless and impulsive spending is often the outcome. Michael describes his experience:

> When I saw that car I knew I had to have it. Its red sporty look was too much for me—it almost didn't matter whether it even had an engine. I managed to get a loan from the bank but I couldn't make the repayments.

Sexual indiscretions

Sexual activity is also influenced by mood. Those who are depressed have little interest in sex, and if this is a particularly important outlet for them they will often consult their doctor about this complaint or blame their partner for their lack of desire. It is not unusual to find, in a marriage with a strained personal relationship or sexual inadequacies, that one or other partner has a depressive mood swing which may prevent them feeling their partner's affection, or dampen their sexual desire.

The heightened sexual desire of elation coupled with the poor judgement that goes with the mood change will often lead to sexual relationships that the person will later regret. To the unsuspecting stranger the elated person will often seem full of vitality, easy in conversation, pleasantly extrovert and downright charming. This new-found charisma will win many a heart and, with the increased sexual desire, may result in hasty marriages, extra-marital affairs and a variety of indiscriminate relationships. Inevitably, these indiscreet liaisons will damage most stable

24

emotional attachments. Joan was a happily married 40-year-old woman, with two teenage children, who always thought she had the perfect marriage:

> I can look back on it all now and see how foolish I had been. It all started after a spell of depression—I had been feeling in top form and was back at work. Somehow I found myself being attracted to a much younger man whom I had worked with for a few years but never really noticed before. I knew what I was doing when I got involved and somehow managed to justify it to myself—not that I can do so now. When my husband found out he was very hurt—he knows now that I was high at the time but it still comes between us and I suppose it always will.

Joan's story is not unusual.

Shoplifting

This can be another outcome of the impaired judgement of those with a mood swing. People who would otherwise be regarded as honest and scrupulous and who would in fact have no need to steal may find themselves before the courts on charges of shoplifting.

In an elated mood the person often seems infused with a sense of dare, they overlook the possible consequences of their actions, such as a court appearance and a conviction for theft and, most surprisingly of all, they are often attracted by the glitter of what they would otherwise regard as worthless trinkets.

During depression the reason for the stealing seems to be even more complex. In some instances it is mainly due to the person's poor concentration and indecisiveness. The depressed housewife who wanders around the supermarket in a bewildered state trying to concentrate on her shopping list, unsure of what to buy, can heedlessly put an item into her pocket rather than into the shopping basket. In other instances the depressed person may take items quite openly in a department store almost as if they wanted to be caught. Here, it appears that they may have strong feelings of guilt and want to be punished, or they may simply want to bring attention to their depression—not everybody when depressed can admit to feeling so and the mind's cry for help must find some other means of expression.

25

Impaired judgement

The impaired judgement of mood swings is often more serious in elation as the person has the drive and enthusiasm to implement their decisions, while in the depressed phase they are protected by their relative inactivity. Driving at high speed, borrowing without giving careful consideration to repayments, signing cheques while having rather unrealistic hopes of having money in the bank to meet their payment and making commitments that can never be kept, are some of the other hazards of elation.

Tricks of the mind

'I'm damned—nobody can save me now' or 'only I can prevent the holocaust that is about to happen'—such are false ideas that often dominate the person's thinking during depression and elation respectively. These delusions or false beliefs are an extension of the negative and positive thinking that are an integral part of the opposite phases of mood swings.

A mildly depressed person will tend to lack confidence in his ability and might think 'I don't seem to do my work very well these days'. As the depression intensifies this line of thinking may progress to 'I'm useless—I can't do anything right and it's my own fault'. In the depths of depression the person will be adamant about his imagined failings and wrongdoings and will attempt to convince others of his total ineptitude. Minor transgressions of his moral code are exaggerated a thousand times, becoming sinful deeds which require comparable retribution. Payment of imagined debts, resignation from work, isolation from family and friends or suicide may be the outcome of their depressive delusions.

Eileen had always considered herself to be a competent teacher until she became depressed. She began to feel that she could not get through to her pupils, doubted her ability to hold their interest and generally felt very self-conscious about her shortcomings. Having discussed the problem with her husband she accepted his assurance that she was being too particular and had no cause to worry. For a time she responded to his encouraging words but gradually became more convinced of her inability to do her work properly, eventually concluding that she was not fit to teach, and

26

that only she really understood this. At times she thought her pupils and colleagues were talking about her incompetence and so she began to avoid them. Finally she resigned from her post before she could be dismissed, utterly convinced that her situation was hopeless.

In elation the shift from grandiose ideas at the outset to firmly held delusions is just as subtle. Martin, who had just returned from a European business trip described his experience thus:

As I became more and more elated I wanted to help people and I felt I had been given a special mission by God. I actually used to lay my hands on sick people I knew or beggars I met in the street, believing that I could cure them. Looking back on it now I know it's ridiculous, but I was so convinced of my healing powers I even began to have visions of the creator—you can imagine how this confirmed my beliefs.

The delusions of manic-depressive illness often occur when the person is in the depths of depression or at the height of an elation and they subside as the mood swing abates. Some of those with more intense delusions also experience auditory and visual hallucinations.

A mood swing will always affect a person's perception of the surrounding world but in most instances this is quite mild. In the depressed phase things look dull and lifeless, and a uniform shade of grey seems to colour their world. Newspapers seem boring, religion is meaningless, and work is unfulfilling and pointless. In elation the very same world is perceived as interesting, colourful and exciting. Paintings take on a new life and meaning and, at times, seem three-dimensional. Music seems captivating and touches the very soul.

These subtle perceptual changes often become more intense as the mood swing intensifies and can result in auditory and visual hallucinations. This might be a voice within the depressed person telling him that he is damned, or a vision occurring during elation in which he might see God giving him a special message about his mission in life. Delusions and hallucinations are terrifying for both patient and relative alike and there is a natural tendency to conceal these experiences, often in the mistaken belief that they indicate a diagnosis of schizophrenia. Perceptual disturbances are not uncommon in depression and elation and differ from the delusions and hallucinations of schizophrenia in that their theme or content is in keeping with the person's mood and that they disappear as soon as the mood swing abates. In schizophrenia the disturbed perceptions are independent of the person's mood change, if any is present, and are not as understandable as those in manic depression. Finally, I must emphasise that those with mood swings who suffer delusions and hallucinations have an equally favourable response to treatment as those without this complication.

Suicide

This is undoubtedly the saddest outcome of a very treatable illness. Should anyone ever doubt the serious nature of depression, they have obviously overlooked the depths of despair that engulf those who contemplate suicide. Some 15 per cent of those with a depressive illness actually take their own lives.

Suicidal thoughts as opposed to actions are very common. Most people have these at some time or other in their lives, usually when everything seems too much and they find themselves 'wishing they weren't here' or half hoping that a passing truck would hit them. Surveys show that such passive wishes occur in some 9 per cent of the general population at any one time.

The sagging confidence, sadness, self-reproach and insurmountable obstacles that depression brings very frequently lead to active suicidal thoughts. In those who are mildly depressed the self-destructive thoughts are fleeting, they are contradicted by day-to-day happenings and the affection of family and friends. As the depression intensifies and their glimmer of hope lessens, they are left with a painful emptiness for which suicide seems the only solution. The risk of a suicide attempt is greatest when the person is emerging from a severe depression. It is as if they lack the initiative and planning ability during the more severe phase of the illness.

Why do people attempt suicide? Most who try to end their lives are, at the time, deeply depressed and the different types of depression provide different explanations for their actions. Anger and frustration are the predominant feelings of those with reactive depression and their self-destructive attempts are frequently aimed at trying to hurt rather than to kill themselves. At other times such a suicidal attempt is meant to punish those who have hurt or disappointed them. Those with the extreme physical pain of a disabling or terminal illness from which they see no reprieve are frequently at risk of suicide.

During a depressive mood swing the sense of emptiness and black despair coupled with extreme mental fatigue are what the person is trying to escape. We very much take for granted our ability to think ahead and project our thoughts into the coming minutes, hours and days. In a severe depressive mood swing this facility is absent and the person is frozen in time in a type of mental vacuum. Everything seems lacklustre and dull, and any thoughts that occur are self-deprecatory and guilt-ridden. In this black pit of depression the person is probably unable mentally or physically to commit suicide, but it is as they emerge from the depths of the depression, still feeling the awful deadness, that they are most at risk.

Those with a severe depression who have little emotional contact in their lives are more likely to attempt suicide. Those who are elderly, widowed, divorced, or live alone often do not have somebody in whom they can confide, somebody to reach out to them in their melancholic void, somebody to contradict their guilt feelings and other depressive distortions.

Most people who commit suicide communicate their intentions to a relative or their doctor and, as such, these warnings must never go unheeded. When talking to a depressed person, if you feel their sense of hopelessness and despair and, in seeing things through their eyes you feel despondent, then they must surely want to escape this black mood. When your best efforts to cheer them up and attempts to show them the positive side of their lot are thwarted it is likely they have reached the ultimate in despair. While a person who is intensely depressed may not actively be contemplating suicide, the degree of despondency he experiences will almost inevitably mean that it has crossed his mind.

What can you do to help? Firstly, always take threats of suicide seriously. Listen to what the person is saying and try to understand how he is feeling. If you can reach them in their misery you have thrown them a lifeline. Do not try to hide the problem or, worse still, call their bluff. It is essential that you get professional help as soon as possible and never attempt to handle the situation yourself. Throughout the depression it is best to give repeated and firm reassurances that they will recover, and encourage them to talk about their feelings. Finally, it is best to avoid alcohol as it may both worsen the depression and precipitate a suicidal attempt.

Conclusion

These complications are the real hazards of mood swings. But they are preventable. Although modern treatments have had a major impact on recurrent mood swings and have lessened the suicide rate, the crucial factor in prevention is the informed patient. Knowing the facts about the illness and its risks, and taking the necessary preventive steps are just as vital as anything your doctor can prescribe.

3

Causes of Mood Swings

In this chapter I shall look at the causes of mood swings, and briefly describe what happens in the brain during a mood change. I shall also discuss the latest research—with its implications for the patient and his family.

Are mood swings inherited?

One of the most striking aspects of manic depression is that it tends to run in families; whereas 1 per cent of the population will develop this illness, some 15 per cent on average of the immediate relatives (parents, brothers, sisters and children) of a person with manic depression will have a mood swing at some time in their lives. But does this necessarily mean that mood swings are inherited rather than acquired?

This question can be answered by two ingenious types of research: twin and adoption studies. Identical twins have exactly the same genetic make-up and so inherited characteristics such as eye colour, which are under genetic control, will be identical. In non-identical twins half of their genetic inheritance will be different from that of the fellow twin and so their eye colour, for example, may be different. On the other hand, when twins have been reared in the same geographical area, they will have the same accent whether they are identical or non-identical twins as accent is an acquired characteristic, determined by cultural factors.

Research of mood swings in twins has produced very interesting results. The essence of these investigations is that if there are 100 pairs of identical twins where one of each pair has mood swings, some 70 of the 100 fellow twins will also have mood swings, whereas in a comparable study of non-identical twins only about 15 of the fellow twins will have a similar mood disorder. In other words, the closer one is genetically related to a person with this disorder the greater the risk of suffering a mood swing.

It might be argued that the very close relationship which exists between identical twins and, thus, their very similar environments, would explain the high rate of mood swings in the fellow twins. However, studies of twins who were separated from birth and reared apart show the same results: the fellow twins of identical pairs with manic depression have a five times higher rate of mood swings than the fellow twins from non-identical pairs whether the pairs were reared together or separately. Furthermore, findings from adoption studies generally concur with these results. They show that the rate of manic depression is considerably higher in the natural than in the adoptive parents of those who have mood swings in adult life. So whether we are prone to mood swings depends to a greater extent on our natural parents than on the environment in which we grew up.

These interesting and clear-cut findings indicate that the reason why mood swings tend to run in families is that they are passed from one generation to the next in the genes. However, this is not the full story. Whereas twin studies show that genetic inheritance accounts for the development of 70 per cent of these mood disorders, in the remaining 30 per cent heredity is not the determining factor. Here, childhood experiences, stress, seasonal variations and other, as yet unknown, influences are the deciding forces.

How do genes produce mood swings?

We get our genes from our parents—they are carried in the egg and sperm. These original cells have long strands of genes on which are dotted various genetic messages which tell the cell what to do, and as these cells produce new cells, each is given the same genetic messages to take with it. Within the cells are factories which respond to the genetic message by making chemicals and structures as ordered. Our body is no more than a collection of these cells, each with its own function. Under instruction from genes, cells specialise, for example, in carrying oxygen (red blood cells), or in transmitting messages (nerve cells). Similarly, a genetic message may instruct the cells to produce pigment, and thus determine the colouring of the skin, or hormones which can circulate around the body.

Within the brain, certain cells are told to control mood but to allow the everyday ups and downs to be felt. They do this by producing certain chemicals which act as messengers. If the mood-controlling gene carries a faulty message this will be conveyed uncorrected to the cells' chemical factories. Here, either the wrong type or amount of mood-controlling neurotransmitters will be produced, resulting in poor control of mood.

Who will inherit these genes?

I previously stated that, on average, 15 per cent of the immediate relatives of those with mood swings will have the same mood disorder. But, of course, some will not have any relative with a mood disorder while others will have more than the 15 per cent average. This means that we cannot accurately predict how many offspring of one individual with manic depression will also develop this illness.

A patient with mood swings who can identify several close family members and relatives from previous generations with a similar disorder, can be presumed, on the basis of twin and adoption studies, to have mainly inherited the illness. Within such families with a strong propensity for mood swings a single gene carrying a faulty message has not been identified. It seems likely that there are several genes involved in controlling moods, and whether these genes ever go on to produce mood swings may be determined by how many of these faulty genes are inherited, how influential are the stabilising effects of the 'normal' genes from the other parent, and whether the person is exposed to the stresses necessary to precipitate a mood change. For those without this family tendency their mood swings are more likely to be due to environmental factors. As you will see later, mood swings are not usually entirely due to either genetic or environmental factors, but to an intricate interaction of both.

What happens in the brain during a mood swing?

The brain is a type of powerful computer specialising in communication. It gathers information from the world about us through our eyes, ears, skin and other sensory detectors. When it has analysed the information it decides whether to simply store it in our memory or to act on it then or later. To carry out these functions the brain has specialised interconnecting nerve cells which bring messages to and from it in the form of minute electrical currents. The mechanism by which we feel pain is a good

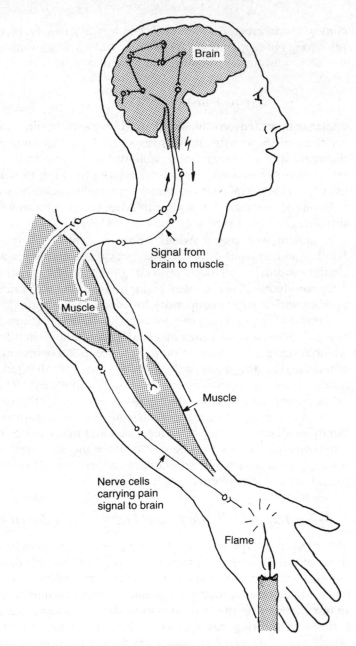

Figure 2: Pain travelling to the brain, which then instructs arm muscles to withdraw the hand from the flame.

illustration of nerve cells at work (see Figure 2 on p. 34). When we put our hand near a flame the heat registers on our skin and a message travels along a chain of nerve cells. The message arriving at the brain's pain centre is then felt as pain. After analysing the signal the brain responds by sending another message down to the arm muscles telling them to recoil the hand from the flame. In a similar manner, vision and sound are transmitted to the brain by our eyes and ears.

Whereas signals travelling along the nerve cells outside the brain usually pass directly from one cell to the next, you will see from Figure 2 that the pattern of communication between the cells within the brain is very much more complex. In fact one brain nerve cell can transmit its signal to as many as a thousand other cells.

The mechanism by which a nerve cell communicates with its neighbouring cells is particularly relevant to mood disorders. An electrical impulse arriving on a cell body passes down the long leg of the cell to its thousand or so feet (see Figure 3 on p. 36). These feet contain numerous stores of chemical messengers which are opened by the electrical signal and emptied into the gap between the foot and the neighbouring cell body. When these messengers arrive at special landing sites on the cell body they set in train further electrical impulses which in turn pass along this nerve cell.

The emotional centre of the brain is a particularly intricate system of interconnecting nerve cells called the limbic system. Here, messages from the outside world and memory interact to stimulate feelings. The smooth control of feelings is dependent on adequately functioning nerve cells and proper amounts of chemical messengers. Extensive research into the chemistry of mood swings suggests that the depressive phase results from a deficiency of one of a number of chemical messengers, or that the landing stations are refusing to accept them. In elation, the chemical messengers are either present in excess, or they are being accommodated in greater numbers on the landing sites.

Two particular chemical messengers, noradrenaline and sero-tonin, are associated with mood swings. Noradrenaline turnover appears to decrease in depression and increase prior to and during elation, while serotonin turnover diminishes in some forms of depressive mood swings and often remains low in elation. How much each of these chemical messengers contributes to individual

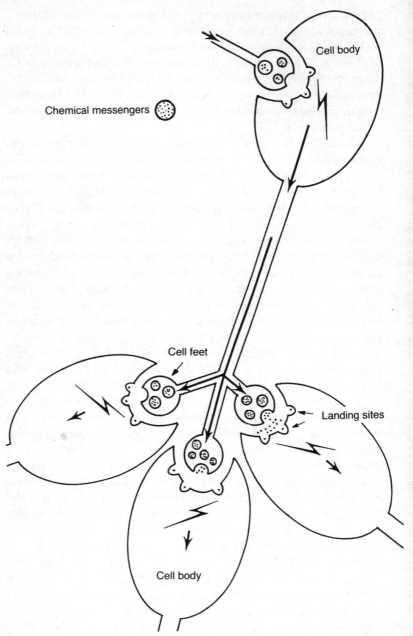

Cell body

Chemical messengers

Cell feet

Landing sites

Cell body

Figure 3: How signals pass from one nerve cell to others within the brain.

mood swings is not clear but some researchers believe that they produce different biochemical types of depression and so will respond to different treatments.

The fluctuating level of chemical messengers may possibly result from 'leaky' nerve cells. Each cell in the body has an outer wall or membrane in which there are tiny pores that can vary in size, and so regulate what passes in and out of it. Research on cells of those with manic depression show that their membranes are defective and, in the case of nerve cells, may result in the leakage of essential chemical messengers.

Are environmental factors relevant?

We saw that for identical twins where one has manic depression, 70 per cent of the fellow twins will have a similar disorder. This left 30 per cent who, despite having the same genetic inheritance, do not develop manic depression. The only possible explanation for this lies in the environment to which the fellow twins were exposed. By environment is meant every influence other than genetic ones and this will include factors such as infections, stress, head injuries, diet, childhood experiences, and so on. A wide range of environmental influences have been investigated and some have furthered our understanding of the causation of mood swings.

Stress and loss

When describing normal depression we saw how most people experience the normal ups and downs of everyday life. One very obvious question that is frequently asked by those who experience a mood swing is whether their mood is due to a recent upset. Stress and loss evoke emotions which often get out of control and result in a reactive depression. A loss in a person's life may take many forms. It may be a death of a close relative, loss of a job or the realisation that a much-desired ambition will never be fulfilled. In effect, anything to which we become attached can, when lost, elicit a sense of despair.

A number of investigations into the effect of loss and stress in depression show that those with depression report three times as many stressful life events before their mood change as does the average person from the same socio-economic background. Also, those who have loss and traumatic events in their lives and become depressed seem to feel more distress before the depression than those who do not become depressed and experience the same degree of loss. It is likely that those who succumb to these unpleasant events lack the high self-esteem and other coping mechanisms of those who weather these upsets. A particular protection against depression is having somebody in whom to confide one's problems; those without a confiding and intimate relationship are more vulnerable to depression.

Despite the effect of personal loss on mood, only some 40 per cent of those admitted to hospital with a depressive mood swing can identify a particular loss or stress which would account for their depression. So while such events are important factors they are not in themselves a sufficient explanation for recurrent mood swings.

A number of researchers have found that, prior to a first episode of depression or elation, the sufferer is more likely to have experienced greater emotional trauma from events such as family illnesses, bereavement, and financial difficulties than the average person, but that for subsequent mood swings the degree of loss and stress is no greater than average. This suggests that upsetting events may switch on the genetic mechanism and the mood swings then become autonomous. Another interesting suggestion is that those with a strong family history of mood swings are more likely to have a mood swing without preceding stress whereas those with only a slight family tendency often develop an episode of elation or depression only after an enormous upset. Two case histories will help illustrate the interaction between upsets and the genetic tendency.

Alice's father and two sisters have had treatment for recurrent depressive mood swings. When she first became depressed she thought that her deteriorating sexual relationship with her husband was the problem, not realising that her falling libido was an early symptom of depression. Since then she has had several episodes of depression which have occurred without an identifiable cause. Alice is now on preventive medication and only rarely gets a mild dip in mood. Obviously, in her instance the inherited tendency to depression was the main, if not the only, causative factor.

John's story is rather different. John is a 37-year-old married

man who works as an insurance agent. He first became elated
when the group with which he played as bass guitarist made a
record. His whole way of life had centred around music and his
only ambition had been to be a successful musician. Prior to each
elation he had been more involved in music than usual, playing
most nights, travelling long distances late at night and arriving
home a few hours before he was due to leave for his office. During
the highs he spoke in a very grandiose manner about his planned
successes. Afterwards he readily accepted that his lifestyle contri-
buted to the mood swing. Sally, his wife, recognised that he was a
very average musician and unlikely to make a reasonable living as
a guitarist. Nor could he afford to give up his insurance job. A
study of John's family showed that a maternal uncle had manic
depression. This indicated that there was a family tendency—but
it was likely that the emotional stress which John's unrealistic
goals were imposing were just as blameworthy for the elations.

Childhood experiences

There is evidence to support the idea that loss of a parent through
death during childhood is associated with depression in later life.
Those who have severe depression in later life have been noted to
be more likely than average to have lost a mother before the age of
eleven years. It is suggested that their depression is an unresolved
grief reaction which erupts under the impact of stress and loss in
adult life. While there is evidence to support an association
between maternal loss and recurrent depressive mood swings,
such an effect has not been implicated in manic depression.

The quality of the early family environment, the parent–child
relationship, family size, and the person's birth position within the
family have been studied in those with mood swings and, although
the results have not been conclusive, a number of interesting
points have emerged. One of these is that the family as a group is
made to feel status-conscious, that the parents emphasise the need
to conform to society's standards and to achieve status. Such
families tend to climb the social ladder, are very conventional, and
place less emphasis on intimacy and interpersonal relationships
than on achievements. The member who becomes ill with mood
swings is often bearing the brunt of the family's ambitions and is
expected to be their standard-bearer. In a sense they are often
seen as being only able to achieve their impossible ambitions in

elation. For them, elation is a last desperate attempt to succeed and depression a realisation of the impossibility of their task.

Seasonal factors

Seasonal variation in the occurrence of mood swings is quite marked, with mania predominating between midsummer and autumn, and depression being more common in the winter months. Minor seasonal shifts in mood are probably universal but are more marked for some people. In certain parts of the world whole communities can experience bouts of lethargy, irritability and sleep disturbance when a particular wind blows. Winds, such as the simoom dust storms from the Sahara desert, the sirocco blowing from North Africa to Sicily and the chinook in Canada, have this mood-altering effect. Various explanations have been offered for this phenomenon. One is that winds alter the level of ionisation or positively charged particles in the atmosphere and that this in turn either influences the level of production of chemical messengers, or the rate of message transmission in the brain's nerve cells. A recent survey finding which would support this theory showed that times of peak admission rates to hospital with mania are associated with periods of low atmospheric humidity. This suggests that ionic changes in the atmosphere may be the seasonally varying factor which can precipitate mood swings.

Other possible explanations for mood variations range from the effect of the lunar cycle to the theory that seasonal mood changes are a carry-over from the animal kingdom, with depression being a form of hibernation and elation representing the heightened activity associated with food storage for the coming winter. Another intriguing possibility is that sunlight has an effect on mood. Light can block the secretion of melatonin, a sleep-inducing hormone produced by the pineal gland in the brain. The theory suggests that in the darker winter months more melatonin is secreted and this then affects the sleep pattern and mood.

Proponents of the ionisation theory recommend using ionisers which will alter the level of ionisation in the home, while melatonin enthusiasts advise phototherapy in the form of intense indoor illumination to simulate spring days in winter. It is too early to say whether these are worthwhile treatments as they both need extensive scientific enquiry.

Miscellaneous factors

Numerous other factors such as vitamin deficiencies, allergies, metal poisoning and low blood sugar have been investigated. To date none have been shown to have a definite causative role. However, medical disorders such as underactivity of the thyroid gland or excess body calcium, medications such as steroids, or anti-hypertensive treatments can produce symptoms which mimic depression and elation.

Conclusion

Mood swings are by and large determined by genetic influences and by a number of as yet unidentified environmental factors. For some, heredity is the only causative factor in this illness, but for others the genetic liability remains dormant until disturbed by one or more of the environmental forces already discussed. The chemical explanation for mood changes is probably extremely complex and it is highly unlikely that it involves just one particular chemical messenger. What is much more likely is that mood disorders result from an imbalance between two chemical messengers, and this imbalance may arise for a variety of different reasons. No doubt when science has unlocked the mysteries of the brain, different types of mood swings will be recognised, just as today the microscope distinguishes between the bacterial, tuberculous and viral types of pneumonia.

Emotions seem to result from a complex interaction between memories, current events and their personal significance. We cannot pretend to understand the nature of the mind, consciousness and those much vaunted human attributes of will-power, perception and judgement. What is abundantly clear is they are easily overrun and made worthless by a severe mood swing. While there is a wealth of research evidence to explain the biological basis of mood swings, this should not be construed as belittling the mysteries of the mind—whose nature is never likely to be explained by present-day scientific concepts.

4

Treatment of Depression and Elation

Here we are concerned with the *treatment* of individual episodes of depression and elation. This must be distinguished from the *prevention* of recurrent mood swings which will be discussed in the next chapter.

Treatment of depression

While the great debate about the place of various drugs, electro-convulsive therapy (ECT) and psychotherapy in the treatment of depression continues, both within and without psychiatry, few would question the enormous value of the anti-depressant medications in the treatment of depressive mood swings. For, more than any other form of depression, the various types of treatment are clearly defined.

We know from the pattern of mood swings that depressions always come to an end of their own accord. What we do not know is how long any individual depression is going to last—it may take weeks or it may take years. What treatment aims to do is to speed the natural recovery process and see the person safely through a most incapacitating illness with a minimum of hurt. For the depressed person, knowing that the black cloud will lift with time is probably the most important lifeline. They will doubt this irrefutable fact and so will need it repeated reassuringly by their relatives and doctor.

Although anti-depressant tablets are very effective alleviators of depressive mood swings, they increase the risk of precipitating elation or greatly accentuating or prolonging what might other-wise be a mild high. So before a person with a mild depressive mood swing is given anti-depressant tablets the benefit of relieving their depression must be weighed against the risk of forging an elation. If depression is relatively mild and the person, having a realistic understanding of the illness, feels able to cope, anti-depressant treatment should be avoided. For more severe depres-sions where despair and despondency dominate, these medic-ations must be used unhesitatingly. The patient who has an informed opinion on the matter can be of great help to their doctor in making therapeutic decisions.

Anti-depressant tablets

Tricyclic anti-depressants. This is a family of drugs introduced in the 1950s; and they remain the preferred treatment for depression. There are several different tricyclic drugs but, as they resemble one another chemically and behave similarly in the body, much of what can be said about one applies to other family members. They are thought to work by enhancing the different neurotransmitters in the brain.

Tricyclic anti-depressants take one to three weeks to work and for some people the wait may be longer. Because of this it is essential to persevere with the treatment. However, most people feel more relaxed and generally sleep better right from the start. If you experience intolerable side-effects tell your doctor. He may advise you to rest for a week or so (during which time the side-effects will peter out), reduce the dosage, or prescribe an alternative treatment.

Amitryptyline (brand names are Tryptizol and Laroxyl) is a potent anti-depressant with some tranquillising effect and can aid sleep if taken at bedtime. *Clomipramine* (brand name is Anafranil) is another effective anti-depressant. It tends to be stimulating and so is useful for those with a sluggish depression. *Trimipramine* (Surmontil) has sedative properties and is very effective for those with marked disruption of sleep. In some instances it can cause nightmares. Other family members include *dothiepin* (Prothiaden), *imipramine* (Tofranil), and *doxepin* (Sinequan).

Side-effects with tricyclics are a problem but rarely sufficient to stop treatment. They can produce dryness of the mouth, blurring of vision, constipation, a slow urine flow, weight gain and impotence. Tremor of the hands and dizziness on standing up quickly may also occur. Most of these symptoms can be minimised by starting with a low dose and gradually increasing as necessary. In the elderly and those with heart disease tricylics can produce irregular heart beats. They seem to be perfectly safe in pregnancy but as a general rule they are best avoided for the first three months. The final risk is that of elation which can be minimised by their cautious use and stopping treatment soon after the depression lifts.

Bill is a middle-aged company accountant who asked for treatment for depression. By nature he had always been a very dynamic and energetic man with numerous interests. For four months or so he had been having a fitful night's sleep, was listless and indecisive and could not concentrate on his work. In his thirties he had a similar depression lasting six months which was successfully treated by his family doctor. On this occasion he had been prescribed tablets but only took them for a few days as they made him drowsy. Understandably, he was reluctant to try medication again. After a detailed explanation of his symptoms and what they were likely to respond to, he agreed to take a course of anti-depressant tablets. By starting with a small dosage, the drowsiness he felt was minimal and after a week he was able to tolerate a full treatment dose. In three weeks he was free of depression, was sleeping well and was getting back to his former hobbies. This is not an uncommon story and emphasises the need to follow your doctor's instructions carefully and persist with treatment.

Second generation anti-depressants. Because of the side-effects of tricylic anti-depressants and their slowness in relieving depression many new drugs, allegedly without these handicaps, have been marketed. *Maprotiline* (Ludiomil), *mianserin* (Bolvidon, Tolvon, Norval) and *viloxazine* (Vivalan) are the principal members. Experience to date suggests that they are rather less effective anti-depressants than the tricyclics and that some of them have as many side-effects.

Monoamine oxidase inhibitors. These are totally different anti-depressants which are particularly useful in depression with phobic or obsessional symptoms. Depressions which are resistant to tricyclic drugs will often respond quite dramatically to these anti-depressants.

Drugs most commonly used in this group are *phenelzine* (Nardil), *Nialamid* (Niamid), *tranylcypromine* (Parnate) and *tranylcypromine with trifluoperazine* (Parstelin). They work by preventing the normal enzymatic digestion of the brain's chemical messengers. One of the big disadvantages of these anti-depressants is that they also block the digestion of certain amino acids present in protein foodstuffs. The amino acids, present in cheese, alcohol and meat extracts and a variety of other foods, can cause an increase in blood pressure which can result in severe headaches, breathlessness and even brain haemorrhage. Cards listing the foods to be avoided are supplied with these tablets and should be carried by the person and shown to any doctor who prescribes other treatment. Provided these precautions are taken the tablets are otherwise mainly free of side-effects and can be literally lifesaving. The risk of elation from monoamine oxidase inhibitors in those with manic depression is much greater than it would be from tricyclics and therefore the former must be used with extreme caution.

Anne's story is a case in point. She had one previous cycle of elation and depression and when she came to her doctor on this occasion she had been going through a lengthy depression. After a course of amitryptyline tablets she felt considerably improved in that she was able to cope with her daily chores, her appetite had improved, and she was able to sleep again. However, she continued to have low patches and her initiative had not returned. As time went on she became impatient and wanted to have the anti-depressant, tranylcypromine, which had previously given her prompt relief from her depression, but her doctor declined to prescribe this because of the risk of elation. Anne had some of these tablets at home and proceeded to take them. A week later she was admitted to hospital with elation. It would have been better in the long run if she had let the residual depression peter out of its own accord rather than resorting to a treatment which carried the risk of inducing elation and so starting off a new mood swing cycle.

Electroconvulsive therapy (ECT)

This unjustly ill-reputed treatment continues to have an important role to play and it remains a reliable and highly effective technique for relieving depression. It is used mainly for severe depressions and those resistant to anti-depressant tablets, where symptoms of weight loss, early-morning wakening, depressive delusions and mental and physical apathy predominate. For some severely depressed patients, to wait three weeks for a response to tricyclic anti-depressants poses too much of a suicidal risk; ECT offers them a quicker recovery.

Today, people who are depressed are less likely to hide their depression, and they tend to seek treatment at an early stage, when treatments such as anti-depressant tablets and psychotherapy will relieve their symptoms. Also, family doctors are in a much better position to treat these problems. For both of these reasons ECT is now used less frequently. Probably those for whom it is most often prescribed are people who have had severe depressions in the past which responded to this treatment and, with a recurrence of their depression they request to have this treatment again as it so promptly relieved them of the disabling mood. When ECT was first introduced it was immediately realised that it could dramatically end depressions which had lasted for years, but the difficulty was knowing what type of depression it was likely to help. Both this and the absence of our present-day effective anti-depressant medication led to it being used for all types of depression and other psychological illnesses. We now know that its use should be reserved for those with severe depressive mood swings and that those with other types of depression will not benefit.

The procedure is quite simple. It involves a mild general anaesthetic injection and, when the patient is asleep, a muscle-relaxing drug is given. Then a low-voltage electric current is applied to both sides of the head simultaneously. This produces a flickering of the eyebrows and a twitching movement of the hands and feet all of which usually last less than one minute. On recovery, the person will be drowsy, may have a headache, but in an hour or so will be able to have a meal.

Research investigations indicate that ECT works by increasing the turnover of chemical messengers in nerve cells and not by the popular myth of erasing the person's depressing memories.

The risks involved with the procedure are minimal and are the same as for any other minor anaesthetic. Memory impairment is the main side-effect and this generally appears after the fourth treatment but recovers soon after the course of treatments has ended. Claims of permanent memory loss and brain damage from ECT have not been confirmed by extensive research studies of memory and intellectual function. Undoubtedly it can impair a person's memory for events occurring around the time of the treatment but these investigations show that memory for prior and subsequent occasions is not any more impaired than if the person did not have this treatment. Those who complain of persistent memory impairment after ECT often have benefited little from the treatment, and their poor recall is often a symptom of a continuing depression.

If your doctor has recommended ECT for you and you have any concern about its use do let him know. He will explain why he has recommended this course of treatment and will discuss the alternatives. On balance, ECT remains a safe and effective treatment for depression and brings dramatic relief to those who are most distressed. The unfounded myths with which it is associated have prevented many very severely depressed patients accepting it, sometimes with fatal consequences.

Psychotherapy

This is a form of therapy in which the doctor, by listening to the patient's account of the emotionally important events and recurrent difficulties in his life, builds up a mental picture of that person. This mental picture helps to explain the origin of the psychological symptoms, lets the person see their blind spot, and thus offers new ways for dealing with the problem.

You will recall Deirdre who, when she was taken advantage of, was unable to speak about her hurt and angry feelings. Instead she became anxious, depressed and panicky. One part of her mind, the emotional side, was made to feel small, insignificant and angry while another part prohibited her from doing anything about these feelings. Throughout her childhood she avoided conflicts and, as her parents advised, espoused the attitude of peace at all cost. She had come to believe that expressions of anger were morally wrong and unfair. Armed with these prohibitions her anger could never be expressed. As an adult she was tempted at times to give vent to her feelings but she was unable to do so as she had never acquired this skill as a child. Through psychotherapy Deirdre became aware of her blind spot, saw how it was the basis of her symptoms, and eventually managed to adopt a more open and assertive approach in her everyday relationships.

For most people, psychotherapy is a bit of a mystery. They find it hard to imagine what their blind spot might be, and for them it is a little like looking for something in the dark; they will know what they are missing when they find it. This talking therapy can be a painful process as past memories and hidden feelings are unearthed, and this is one reason why it can only proceed at what

47

some would think a slow pace.

There are many forms of psychotherapy, ranging from 'brief' psychotherapy which may involve eight one-hour therapy sessions to psychoanalysis, which may entail daily sessions for a number of years. These days most psychotherapists use a variety of different psychological approaches depending on the problem at hand. Rather than sitting back and letting the process move at its own pace, as in Freudian psychoanalysis, the therapist is likely to be more active, ask questions, direct the dialogue and suggest possible ways of resolving the emotional conflicts.

Cognitive therapy. A more recently introduced treatment for depression is 'cognitive therapy'. This is based on the idea that a person's emotions are determined by their thinking and that the sadness and guilt of depression are due to faulty thinking. The person who thinks little of himself will often find that he is on the lookout for similar hints from those around him. In this frame of mind they are likely to be only able to register negative comments, ignoring praise and other positive remarks. Their poor self-image may be nothing more than a collection of negative thoughts accumulated over the years. When eventually they become depressed it is often as a result of some minor mishap which they believe confirms their worst thoughts about themselves. Cognitive therapy is aimed at getting them to recognise their automatic negative thoughts and to see the connection between these, their bad feelings and depressive behaviour. With practice a person can learn to substitute more realistic thoughts once the negative trend has been spotted.

Group psychotherapy. Another form of psychotherapy for depression is group psychotherapy. This usually consists of a group of eight to twelve people meeting on a weekly basis with a therapist. Although members of the group may have different psychological problems they can learn much about the origins of their symptoms when they understand how they interact with the therapist and other members of the group. A group meeting regularly becomes a type of family, and the therapist facilitates members to explore their feelings, and understand the way in which they communicate with one another. As members become more aware of their blind spots they will develop healthier means of coping with day-to-day life outside the group setting. When this form of therapy is first recommended to patients they may consider it to be second best, preferring direct contact with their doctor. It is in fact a very practical way of recreating complex interpersonal relationships with other people who will evoke a variety of different emotions and psychological responses. As such, it has a distinct therapeutic role quite different to that of individual psychotherapy.

Use of psychotherapy. Psychotherapy is the preferred approach for those with reactive and neurotic depressions. It has no useful function in the acute stage of manic-depressive illness or in a depressive mood swing with endogenous features where there is no clear-cut precipitating event. In these depressive mood swings psychotherapy can be dangerous if it releases painful memories that the person's already overstretched coping mechanisms are unable to manage. Usually such depressed minds are inaccessible to these forms of treatment. However, once the mood change has abated it is very worthwhile exploring any recurrent thoughts or preoccupations that were of concern during the mood swing. Likewise, focusing on the events that may have precipitated the depression can often be revealing; for example, a person may know that their depression followed an argument but be quite puzzled why they responded by becoming depressed until they understood the emotional significance of the dispute. Meanwhile doctors, nurses, psychologists or social workers who are involved with depressed patients can do much to support the depressed person by offering a regular sympathetic hearing, explaining the nature of the illness and, most importantly, by giving repeated assurance about the outcome.

Depression: advice for patients

It is hard to see depression as an illness as it very often starts in an imperceptible manner and the effect it has on thinking subtly changes your usual outlook. There will be no flashing lights when the depression descends. The best way to spot it in its early stages is to note the symptoms which you experienced previously, and if you have forgotten, those described in Chapter 2 may help your recall. Tiredness is probably the commonest subjective symptom of a depressive mood swing. Other useful indicators are reduced activity in the form of being reluctant to tackle work, avoiding social gatherings and a lessening involvement in leisurely pursuits.

Having recognised the mood change do not try to hide it. You will find it hard to admit what is happening to you but it is not advisable that you manage it on your own. Talk to a relative or a friend in whom you would usually confide—I am sure you would wish them to do likewise if positions were reversed.

If this is the first time that you have had a depressive mood swing do remember that it is a very treatable condition. Confide in your doctor, tell him how you are feeling and what worries you. He will be able to advise you appropriately and the information you give him will be of help in deciding what treatment, if any, is necessary. If you are having difficulty in talking to your doctor or feel he is unsympathetic, do let him know. The doctor-patient relationship is a personal matter and is a very necessary component for successful treatment. Your doctor will want to know if there is something interfering with this working alliance and thus possibly impairing your recovery. Together you can explore what has gone wrong and you will almost invariably find a solution to the problem. If he has prescribed anti-depressant tablets and you find you are having side-effects do not forget that these will usually fade in a week or so and the anti-depressant effect will then become apparent. Knowing when to stop these tablets is sometimes difficult; if the treatment is discontinued too soon the depression may re-emerge, whereas prolonged use may result in elation. In this decision it is best to be guided by your doctor, and perhaps have the treatment gradually relaxed under his supervision. Never try to do this alone and without his knowledge.

Being depressed, you probably feel tired and find it a great effort to do most things. Generally it is best to keep as active as you can. Then, at the end of the day, even if you have just managed to get dressed and potter about, it will be a comfort to know that you have been able to do this. Aim only to do the essentials, avoid intellectual tasks and, if possible, do not undertake new jobs. However, if despite your best efforts you are getting nowhere it is best to sit out the depression; your fruitless efforts will only tend to heighten your sense of inadequacy.

How long should you wait before consulting your doctor if you feel down? If the depressive symptoms last more than a week it is advisable to get medical help. However, if they are particularly severe do so right away. Recognise the symptoms for what they are and do not pretend that they are not happening. George's story emphasises this point. He is a farm worker who has been getting depression every winter for the past ten years. For the first few years he was always caught off guard, being convinced each time that the depression would not return. As a result his depressions were well advanced when he sought treatment and he usually needed to go to hospital. Now, when he realises that he has been unusually tired, is waking during the night and is not interested in his fishing magazine, he knows that he is slipping into a depression. For the past three winters he has managed to curtail the mood swing by contacting his doctor when he sees the warning signs, and starting anti-depressant medication at an early stage.

Alcohol should be avoided; it can make the depression worse, release suicidal thoughts and interact with the anti-depressant tablets to make you drowsy and unsteady. It is important to postpone making major decisions during a depression. Those who make significant alterations, believing that they will bring relief, often have regrets when their perception is no longer clouded by their mood.

Depression: advice for relatives

It is usually obvious if a person close to you is severely depressed, but he can manage to conceal it in the early stages when he still can wear a smile or pretend to be cheerful. As the depression progresses, along with the usual signs and symptoms I have previously listed, you will notice that he withdraws from you emotionally, leaving you feeling shut out. If he has had depressions before, you will probably have your own familiar warning signs. Most depressions start gradually and, as such, you should endeavour to get the person to talk about his feelings early on as he will be more accessible at this point. Once you have assessed the extent of his depression you have to use your judgement on how urgent the problem is. If the person is severely depressed persuade him to see his doctor immediately. In milder mood swings, with a gradual onset, there is no urgency. If you know from previous experience the rate at which the depression develops and how much it can influence the person's judgement then you will know what to do. Whatever else, do not undertake to treat the mood swing yourself. While you may know most of the facts and will undoubtedly be able to be of assistance, do remember that depression is a complex matter requiring professional help.

You may have been the person who made the patient visit the doctor in the first place. Depressed people are often reluctant to do most things and in this sense you must give them some guidance. You can be an important link between patient and doctor by ensuring that the tablets are taken as prescribed, that the person avoids making major decisions and by reinforcing the doctor's assurances of a good outcome. If well-meaning relatives or friends tell the patient to 'snap out of it' or 'pull yourself together' discourage this kind of pressure as it is unkind and can be harmful. A sympathetic and understanding attitude is needed throughout. While waiting for the treatment to take effect your contact can be a lifeline to a depressed person, encaged as he is in an emotional vacuum. You should encourage him to remain active, if necessary by sharing some of his chores. If you find that your best efforts are futile and are not making any impact then the depression has reached a dangerous stage.

Suicidal thoughts occur in most cases of depression and should you feel the patient is thinking about this or talks about it let the doctor know. He will advise on the necessary precautions. Talk of suicide must always be taken seriously. Constant reassurance is a great comfort and helps counter the patient's despondent and negative thoughts, and your role is crucial in this respect. If you think that you cannot watch over the person as he becomes more severely depressed and thus limit the risk of suicide, then he is best off being cared for in hospital.

Treatment of elation

Whereas a depressive mood swing needs treatment in its own right, elation, by contrast, frequently has to be interrupted because of the serious nature of its complications. The person is often unaware of his altered mood state, particularly when it happens for the first time, and so may vehemently resist attending a doctor and decline treatment. Then the responsibility falls to relatives who have to contend with a person whose judgement is gradually deteriorating and who is acting out of character. Eventually this may result in the person being compulsorily admitted to hospital by the family to prevent the complications of elation.

In its mildest form the person may simply need advice to avoid the potential hazards. If the mood change is more pronounced and the person has a realistic understanding of the need for treatment, tablets can be prescribed without recourse to hospitalisation. Allowing a trusted relative or friend to monitor the mood change and liaise with the doctor usually ensures a successful outcome.

Anti-elatant tablets

Phenothiazines. These drugs were first introduced in 1952 and since then many members have been added to the family. While their action is not specifically anti-elatant they have a profoundly sedative effect in mania. As with tricyclic antidepressants, the phenothiazine family members have much in common; they share a similar chemical structure, and have the same mechanism of action and side-effects. Within the brain they prevent the chemical messengers landing on the cell bodies by occupying their 'landing' sites.

Chlorpromazine (Largactil) is the elder member of the family and is a powerful sedative. Its calming effect is felt within a half hour and lasts for about eight hours. Other closely related drugs are *promazine* (Sparine) and *thioridazine* (Melleril).

Haloperidol (Serenace, Haldol) is a more potent anti-elatant than chlorpromazine. It has a rapid effect on racing thoughts and overactivity. As it is not particularly sedative it is frequently used in combination with chlorpromazine. The dosages of each are increased until they have the desired calming effect.

The main side-effects of these drugs involve the body muscles. Normal spontaneous movements of the face, arms and other muscles are diminished, producing a stiff appearance and drooling of saliva. Restlessness in the legs, which limits the length of time a person can stand or sit in the one place, can also occur. Another effect is a sudden locking of muscles of the face or tongue. All of these side-effects, although distressing, are readily kept to an imperceptible level and are counteracted by another tablet, *benztropine* (Cogentin), or *orphenidrine* (Disipal). Other side-effects of phenothiazines are drowsiness, blurred vision and rashes. Largactil has an additional handicap in that it can cause a severe sunburn reaction in those exposed to the sun.

Lithium. While the phenothiazines dampen elation without

altering its duration, lithium dramatically limits its length. Another major advantage is that it is relatively free of side-effects. However, as it takes 10–14 days to take effect, haloperidol and chlorpromazine are often necessary to control the mood in the meantime. Details of lithium treatment, how it behaves in the body and its side-effects will be found in Chapter 5.

Elation: advice for patients

Recognising elation is often difficult. This is because it is usually a pleasurable experience and, as such, does not immediately strike you as needing treatment. So it is important to take a few precautions. Realising that you would want the elation treated is the first step. Those who find it a pleasurable mood can, if they wish, ignore the way it disrupts their own and their family's lives, forget about the depression that usually follows, and so choose to avoid treatment. I have yet to meet somebody who, after taking all the consequences of the elation into account, wanted to continue to have this seemingly pleasurable mood. Those who refuse to limit their 'highs' have usually not fully understood its effects.

Having decided that you want to limit the elation, the next step is to detect it in its early stages. To do this you must first accept that you may not be able to spot it. However, a close relative or friend will notice the change in mood early on and you should ask them to alert you to this. It is essential that you let some close confidant get involved in spotting the illness otherwise you may find that when it is detected you will need to be admitted to hospital. If you have previously been elated ask a relative to help you in this respect as they may well be reluctant to intervene lest you take offence. This may mean granting them permission to ensure that you see your doctor, to remove your cheque book or car keys, or whatever else they think is in your best interest at the time. They can provide a very necessary safety net.

Many who have had a previous episode of elation recognise it when it recurs. If the mood change has been unpleasant then the person is likely to seek help immediately. Most people, though, will need to be more vigilant as the change from normal mood to elation is relatively imperceptible. Many of the symptoms go unnoticed, but some, such as racing thoughts, difficulty in getting off to sleep, and a feeling of being very busy, are useful warning signs. A person will often find that as they become elated they do something out of character which, in itself, is harmless, but which family members come to recognise as a tell-tale sign. One person I know who had been a lifelong non-smoker always starts to smoke, and another wears a very distinctive pair of red socks at the start of each elation.

Clive's history is an all too familiar account. He first became elated when on a holiday with his family in the Far East. Prior to that he had been away on a business trip and his wife, Maura, had been hoping that the holiday would be an opportunity for them to be together. Instead she found he was restless, could not relax, and that they argued a lot. He began to drink more than usual, was noisy and truculent late at night, and eventually clashed with the hotel manager. Clive felt that he was being treated unfairly by all and when the police were called to break up a fight he had started, he was even more arrogant. It was when he landed in jail that Maura realised that this was not the Clive she knew and asked that he be seen by a doctor. He was subsequently sent home for treatment and made a good recovery. Two years later he had another manic mood and was just as slow to accept that he was ill. When his mood had abated he was fortunate to meet others with this problem at group therapy sessions. He learned from them the need to take preventive action and to allow his wife to become involved in the treatment. Since then Clive and Maura have experienced at first hand that they can recognise the mood swings at an early stage, limit their complications, and prevent the need for hospital admission.

When you are first told by your family that you are 'high', or your doctor diagnoses elation you may understandably feel annoyed, puzzled and unable to accept that there is anything wrong. Many have travelled this road before you, some have had to learn the hard way and experience some of the complications of elation before they realised they needed treatment. Others have been able to take their family's word and doctor's advice, so minimising the problem. Financial debts, marital disruption and the many other problems associated with elation cannot always be undone afterwards—so be guided by someone you have found to be trustworthy in the past.

If you experience a recurrence of elation do not pretend it is not happening. Hopefully you will be able to recognise the early warning signs and take appropriate action. It is a good idea to have a plan on how to manage the situation. This might involve taking definite steps to limit your spending power, avoiding situations which you know have a stimulating effect on your mood, declining to get involved in new ventures, or whatever you and a close relative consider necessary. It is best not to take alcohol; it often fuels the mood change and interferes with the anti-elatant medication. Physical exercise can have a calming effect and is to be recommended if taken in moderation.

Early medical advice and treatment will lessen the interruption to your life and frequently prevent the need for admission to hospital. As with depression, it is wise to keep your family and doctor informed about how you feel, as any medication you are taking will need to be altered as the elation subsides.

Elation: advice for relatives

Elation is undoubtedly the most difficult aspect of the illness from your point of view. If the patient adamantly rejects that there is anything wrong with his behaviour, it may be impossible to avoid a confrontation. Remember this is an illness over which he may have limited control and as his judgement is impaired you may be the only one who stands between him and a calamity. If the person, despite your best efforts, remains unwilling to seek help, talk to your doctor. He may be able to convince the person to accept treatment or, failing this, will have to recommend compulsory admission to hospital. Despite the understandable anger of the person who is certified, they nearly always accept the correctness of this procedure when the elation ends. Hopefully matters will not reach such a crisis point, but unfortunately they frequently do for the first or second bout of elation.

If you notice an elation beginning but it is as yet quite mild, it is best to mention it to the person. However, if the person is unaware of the change be careful how you word it. None of us likes hearing things about ourselves which are obvious to others but of which we are totally unaware. So a tentative approach is best rather than 'accusing' them of being elated. Do remember that elation is not a self-induced state or a form of wanton waywardness. It is an illness and you should endeavour to be objective and non-judgemental.

When Maura realised that Clive had changed she was convinced that he had turned against her. She felt that his demanding and inconsiderate manner meant that he had lost his affection for her.

As his behaviour became more out of character she realised that he must be ill and found him medical help. What she found hard to accept was that he could not see the elations and, in fact, seemed to enjoy his highs. With each mood swing she had to confront him about his overspending, reckless manner and the way he was upsetting their children. Having him compulsorily admitted to hospital was the most difficult step of all, but she knew that if she did not get him to have the necessary treatment she would end up leaving him.

When the patient with elation visits the doctor your account of his activities will be very helpful in assessing the extent of the mood change. Very often, in the formality of a doctor's surgery, the person is reasonably quiet and less overtalkative and so it may be difficult for the doctor to assess accurately the severity of the mood change. So your objective report of how the patient is faring and whether there are difficulties with the medication is essential for a successful treatment.

Any help that you can give the patient to refrain from overspending or making drastic decisions, and to keep them out of circulation until the elation has abated, will be invaluable.

5

Preventing Recurrences

While one bout of elation or depression will cast a temporary gloom, for those dragged from pillar to post by recurrent mood swings life becomes a waking nightmare. Bout after bout shatters their confidence and often deprives them of family and friends without any hope of a lasting reprieve. Anti-depressants and anti-elatants lessen their hurt and contain the emotional upheaval of each episode as it arises, but do nothing to hinder recurrences. Over the past twenty years extensive research has shown that lithium can dramatically counter recurrent mood swings and it is rightly considered one of the foremost discoveries of twentieth-century medicine. Those who experienced manic depression before the introduction of lithium have seen their moods replaced by a life of normality; more recent sufferers have been spared the full wrath of this tragic illness and its several complications.

Any long-term illness, be it diabetes, hypertension or manic depression, is initially met with denial by the patient. Although the person is fully aware of the diagnosis they have not fully accepted the implications of the illness and may stop their treatment or disregard the dietary and other advice. This emotional rebellion is understandable. Lithium, although it is the cornerstone of preventive treatment, will be of little use if it is not taken as prescribed or if the person, while reluctantly complying with treatment, continues to resent the illness in a manner that distorts their view of life.

Lithium: the mood stabiliser

When the Australian psychiatrist John Cade first used lithium in 1949 he found it calmed manic patients. It was at a later stage that its more important preventive value was realised. Lithium is a natural element much like sodium in table salt and is found in certain rocks, mineral waters and plants. Although present in the human body in minute amounts it has no known physiological function and does not appear to be needed for normal health.

How the body handles lithium

Think of the body as being a tank of water which, in a sense, it is; the fluid portion of the body is more than half its total weight. When lithium tablets are taken by mouth they dissolve into little particles in the stomach and pass into the bloodstream; from there they are carried to all parts of the body. Lithium escapes from the body through the kidneys into the urine; this filtering process tends to be slow so there is a tendency for lithium to build up in the bloodstream. Within the body, lithium competes for space with another particle, like lithium, called sodium; when there is little sodium in the system, lithium has free rein and is less likely to be pushed out through the kidneys.

Research has shown that a certain amount of lithium is necessary to prevent mood swings; if a person has a low blood lithium he will continue to have relapses. Also it is relatively easy to have too much lithium in the body, which gives rise to unpleasant toxic effects. Compared with other tablets such as antibiotics or mild analgesics, the gap between too much and not enough lithium is very narrow. For this reason the amount in the body has to be monitored by regularly measuring the blood lithium level. So by altering the dose of lithium tablets being taken, the blood level can be brought within the therapeutic range (see Figure 4 on p. 60). The standard lithium blood test is taken in the morning twelve hours after the last lithium tablet of the night before. If the blood sample is taken before or after this interval a higher and lower blood lithium concentration, respectively, will be obtained. In practice it is reasonable to have the blood sample taken between eleven and thirteen hours after the last lithium tablet.

Why might the concentration of lithium in the body rise and produce toxic effects? One reason is that if too many lithium tablets are taken, the kidney filters are unable to clear the backlog. Secondly, if the kidney filters stop working because of some kidney disease the blood lithium level will similarly increase. Finally, when the body is depleted of sodium there will be more room for lithium and so its concentration increases. Sodium deficiency occurs when the body loses it through vomiting, diarrhoea, very profuse sweating or diuretic tablets and when there is insufficient intake of sodium due to a poor appetite, a slimming diet, or a low-salt diet.

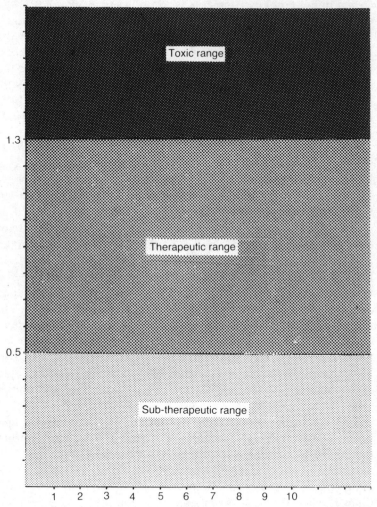

Figure 4: Lithium Therapeutic Range

Lithium tablets are best taken at intervals throughout the day rather than at one time. If, for example, all of the tablets are taken in the morning the blood level may be above the therapeutic range initially and will go below this range towards the end of the day. If, on the other hand, the tablets are taken at eight-hourly intervals a smoother blood lithium pattern will be obtained within the therapeutic range (see Figure 5 on p. 62). As with many other effective treatments, exactly how lithium works is not known. The best explanation we have is that within the brain it regulates the production, storage and release of the chemical messengers implicated in recurrent mood swings, or limits their impact at nerve cell landing sites.

Practical aspects of lithium treatment

Before lithium is prescribed for its long-term preventive use it must be clearly established that the patient is likely to benefit—in other words, that he can expect to have further relapses without preventive measures. For those who have had three or more definite mood swings the risk of further episodes is very high. In general, preventive lithium is prescribed for those who have had two to three bouts of manic-depressive illness over the same number of years. However, these rules must take account of each patient's social and economic circumstances. Sometimes it may be advisable for a person who has had just one bout of severe elation to take lithium for one to two years if, for example, a further manic swing after a short interval would almost certainly mean the end of a marriage or unemployment.

The next step is to ensure that the person is medically fit and that their kidneys will be able to handle lithium. This involves having a general physical examination, a blood sample to check that kidneys and thyroid gland are functioning normally and a urine test. Other investigations may be necessary depending on the person's general physical health.

Presuming that all is well medically, lithium will be prescribed in gradually increasing doses over a few weeks until its concentration in the blood, as measured by the standard 'twelve hour' lithium blood test, is within the therapeutic range. Once a satisfactory and stable blood level has been achieved the dose producing this blood level will continue to be prescribed. Treatment will need to be taken indefinitely as lithium does not cure the illness but simply

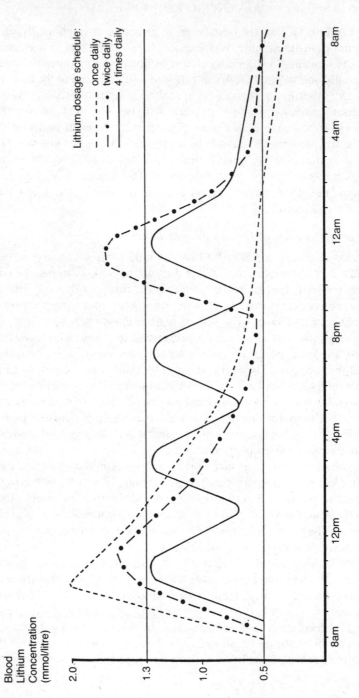

Figure 5: The effect of different dosage schedules on blood lithium concentration

prevents it recurring. This fact is highlighted by one study which reported that 80 per cent of those who had been taking lithium for a number of years relapsed within a year of having their treatment stopped, and the majority of these did so within six months.

It is necessary for those on maintenance treatment to have a lithium blood test taken at least every three months, and the general blood and urine tests detailed above at six-monthly intervals. This will allow any change in the body's handling of lithium to be detected at an early stage. Routine monitoring of blood changes, lithium blood levels and general medical investigations are most conveniently carried out at a 'lithium clinic', specifically set up for this purpose. Here a patient will meet others with the same illness, and they will have the opportunity to discuss their mutual problems and learn from each other's experience.

Lithium treatment during pregnancy and the post-natal period

Lithium increases the risk of congenital malformation in the unborn child. The first three months of pregnancy is the crucial time for foetal development; for the remaining two-thirds of the pregnancy lithium can be taken with safety. Women of child-bearing age who are taking lithium must take contraceptive precautions. If a woman in such circumstances wants to start a family she should discuss the matter with her doctor who will advise her appropriately. It may be possible for her to have the first three months of the pregnancy coincide with that time of year when she is least likely to have a mood swing. As soon as a woman on lithium discovers she is pregnant she should report to her doctor.

While lithium can be recommended after the first three months of pregnancy, frequent monitoring of the blood lithium concentration is necessary as the kidneys excrete it more rapidly during the second half of pregnancy. The rate of excretion then drops to the pre-pregnancy level as soon as the baby is born.

Lithium passes from the mother's blood into the milk and so babies who are breastfed can have a blood lithium concentration as high as half of that of the mother. This means choosing either breastfeeding and interrupting lithium therapy, or bottle-feeding which allows the treatment to continue.

Unwanted effects of lithium

These can be conveniently divided into two categories; side-effects which occur when blood lithium level is within the therapeutic range, and toxic effects when the blood lithium level is above the therapeutic range. While the former are mild and innocuous, the latter are serious — hence the need for regular monitoring of the blood lithium level.

Within the therapeutic range, the more common side-effects are a fine tremor, polyuria (increased flow of urine), polydypsia (increased intake of fluid) and weight gain which is often due to drinking high-calorie drinks to relieve thirst. Less frequently encountered side-effects are mild memory impairment and tiredness, both of which are more likely indicative of a mild depression. Lithium will often exacerbate acne and psoriasis. Most of these unwanted effects can usually be relieved by reducing the blood lithium level within the therapeutic range. Prolonged treatment with lithium can induce a goitre (swelling of the thyroid gland in the neck) or underactivity of the thyroid gland. This can be easily rectified by adding a thyroid hormone tablet to the treatment and it is not a sufficient reason for stopping lithium.

Toxic side-effects occur when the blood lithium concentration is above 1.3 millimoles per litre (a millimole is a measurement of the amount of substance, in this instance lithium). Initially the person will experience drowsiness and tiredness with an inability to concentrate. They will have a marked tremor of the hands, unsteady gait, slurred speech, nausea, vomiting and diarrhoea. If any of these symptoms emerge they should be brought to the doctor's attention immediately because the lithium level may continue to rise and the patient may lapse into coma.

Lithium, being a natural element, is not a drug in the usual sense. No matter how many years the treatment has been taken the person never becomes immune to its benefit. Neither can they become addicted to its use. If a person relapses when lithium treatment is stopped it simply means that the underlying illness has re-emerged rather than that the person is having withdrawal symptoms.

Lithium tablets

Lithium is available as conventional tablets and in a slow-release form. While the latter should allow the tablets to be taken twice rather than four times daily, some so-called slow release tablets do not in fact act as such. The conventional tablets dissolve quickly in the stomach and thus are more rapidly absorbed. The slow release preparations should produce a smoother lithium level and therefore fewer unwanted effects. On the other hand they are often incompletely absorbed and cause diarrhoea when they reach the lower bowel. A list of the more widely available lithium preparations is shown in Table 1.

Table 1: *Lithium Tablets*

Brand Name	Chemical Name	Quantity per Tablet	Type
Camcolit	lithium carbonate	250mgs and 400mgs	Conventional
Liskonum	lithium carbonate	450mgs	Slow Release
Litarex	lithium citrate	564mgs	Slow Release
Phasal	lithium carbonate	300mgs	Slow Release
Priadel	lithium carbonate	400mgs	Slow Release

Effectiveness

While lithium has a tremendous impact on the prevention of mood swings it does not help everyone with this illness. Several investigations have shown that about 75 per cent of patients have an excellent response in that they do not have further mood swings. Another 15 per cent have limited benefit in that they continue to have mood swings but these are less intense and briefer than before. The remaining 10 per cent have no therapeutic response. Which of these groups the patient belongs to will often not be apparent until at least the end of the first year of treatment when a comparison of the mood frequency of the year before and the year of treatment can be made. Lithium is an effective, although by no means an ideal, mood stabiliser. Such is the improvement in the quality of their lives for those who benefit from this treatment that they are usually more than happy to continue taking the tablets despite their mild side-effects.

Michael is one of the many who have benefited from this treatment. After two elations and three depressions he has been free of mood swings since he started on lithium five years ago. He notices that he has some difficulty getting off to sleep each August—the time of year that he had his elations—but is otherwise without symptoms. He lives a full and active life with his family and has returned to his work in computer sales. He can live with what has happened and accepts that he must continue with the medication if he is to be free of mood swings. Four times a year he visits his doctor for a check-up and he does not consider that either this or taking lithium interferes unduly with his life.

Joan likewise feels that she has benefited from preventive treatment. She no longer gets the dreaded elations during which she did many 'crazy' things, and her depressions have become both less severe and less frequent. For three weeks or so each winter she feels dispirited, tired and anxious and she knows this to be a slight depression. With some minor adjustments to her treatment she is quickly over this limited mood swing.

While the use of lithium for prevention of alternating moods of elation and depression has been substantiated for a number of years its effect on recurrent depressive mood swings has only recently been confirmed. Research trials indicate that both lithium and amitryptyline (Laroxyl, Tryptizol) are equally effective in preventing depressive mood swings and that there is little to choose between them. However, if a person who has been diagnosed as having recurrent depressions is in fact having mild elations which go undetected, being on an anti-depressant such as amitryptyline may make what was a mild elation worse. Whether an anti-depressant or lithium is prescribed depends on the side-effects the patient has previously encountered with these treatments, whether mild elations can be positively excluded and how feasible it is for them to have regular lithium blood tests.

Andrew is a 37-year-old store worker who has had a chequered career because of depression. He first had a severe depression in his mid-teens which was treated in hospital. At that time he was advised to leave school and pursue manual work. Almost every year since then he had a prolonged depression which he usually attributed to some problems at work. He lost several jobs because of lengthy periods of sick leave. His depressions in fact had all the hallmarks of a depressive mood swing, occurring in the winter months and usually without any meaningful stress. Andrew has been free of these moods since he started taking amitryptyline on a regular basis. Each October he can now run a marathon rather than be bed-bound with depression.

For those failing to respond to lithium, other drugs with mood-stabilising properties such as *carbamazepine* (Tegretol) and *flupenthixol* (Fluanxol, Depixol) are being studied and show some promise. Carbamazepine has been recently used for mood swings of depression and elation which have been partially or totally resistant to lithium. It is mainly prescribed to prevent epileptic convulsions but its mood-stabilising property would appear to be a separate function. This medication seems to be particularly helpful for those with very frequent mood swings and may be prescribed on its own or combined with lithium. Its anti-elatant effect is apparent within days but it takes up to three weeks to relieve depression. Side-effects encountered are dizziness, unsteadiness, rashes and, very rarely, it can lower blood cell production. How effective carbamazepine will be in preventing mood swings will have to be extensively researched before it becomes a well-established treatment.

Psychotherapy

While lithium is without doubt the most effective preventive for recurrent mood swings, supplementary psychotherapy can be useful. After an episode of depression or elation it is often worthwhile exploring the thoughts which were of concern during the mood swing. This will often reveal unresolved grief, inappropriate guilt feelings or unrealistic ambitions. Discussing these matters at a time when the patient's mood is stable will often allow their realistic assimilation and thus reduce the possibility of further mood swings. Problems of day-to-day living and the patient's social and psychological environment may contribute to their ongoing illness and these must be given due attention.

Bill's story emphasises how psychotherapy can help. Since he left school five years ago he has been mainly unemployed. He started to train as a supermarket manager but after a few weeks felt it was pointless as he was never going to become a millionaire that way. Each time he became elated he talked about his grandiose plans for making money, would sometimes try to organise a pop concert but never made much headway. Although his mood swings abated with lithium he continued to fantasise about making his fortune, yet never attempted to institute any of his schemes. Over a number of psychotherapy sessions he talked about his need to feel successful and how he never had been able to face the possibility that he might fail. Rather than pursue more realistic goals at which he might fail he chose to daydream about plans which he knew he would not attempt and therefore never be

67

seen to fail. He began to see how his thinking was in a permanent cul-de-sac. When he managed to tackle small tasks for which he was paid he gradually began to be freed of his unrealistic thinking. Now he is happy with his lot and is not as afraid to fail.

Anne also benefited from psychotherapy. Her response to lithium had been disappointing in that her mood swings continued to recur although they were of shorter duration. She had always had a sense of inadequacy which she described as like having a little man inside her head muttering negative thoughts about her all day long. Anne tended to compensate for her inferiority feelings by taking on additional tasks at work, by trying to be a super mother and helping out with local charities. In fact she was never idle. Sooner or later she would become overstretched with her self-imposed load and become elated. When she examined the motives for her compensatory activity it became clear that she had always striven to please her father but could never do so. She was made to feel second-rate even though she had excelled in many endeavours. There was always something that could be improved. With this insight into her difficulties she plucked up her courage and spoke to her father. She was quite surprised at his response. He told her that he thought very highly of her, accepted that he should have said so over the years and confided that he also found it hard to see himself in a favourable light. Since then Anne has been able to say good things about herself and resist the temptation to return to her old ways.

Psychotherapy in itself is not sufficient to control mood swings but it is often necessary for those who tend to repeat their mistakes and leave themselves vulnerable to further stresses which in turn precipitate another round of mood changes.

Coming to terms with the illness: the other half of prevention

Illness is never part of man's dream—most of us dare not ever think of it. When it intrudes into our lives our responses will vary from despairing indifference to downright rage. Conflicting as it does with our aspirations, a mental battle follows in which we attempt to deny the reality of what is happening and continue to live life as before. For mild and self-limiting illnesses such as the common cold or muscle strain this may be a healthy response. For others, such as hypertension, it is dangerous. It is not unusual for those who are told that they have high blood pressure to reject treatment and later to develop life-threatening complications. Likewise with manic depression; by its nature it tends to recur and needs long-term preventive treatment; otherwise the person faces a very unstable future with the many hazards of the illness.

If you are only going to have one mood swing cycle then the problem of acceptance and the need for preventive treatment does not arise. For the 50 per cent or so whose mood swings recur, adaption is very necessary as the illness will not go away of its own accord. Even for those who know they have benefited from mood-stabilising medication, the possibility of a further mood swing must not be lost sight of as it tends to lead to haphazard taking of tablets and an inevitable relapse. Each person has got to come to terms with the reality of the illness or risk the possibility of being buffeted from year to year by turbulent moods. With the aid of some case histories, let us examine the various steps to acceptance.

Heeding the reality of the recurrent mood disorder takes time and understanding. Most are deeply numbed when first given the facts, and at a later stage react angrily to their predicament. Marcia had an elation for five consecutive summers. It usually happened when she was abroad on holiday and continued in the same vein on her return. She spent her days leaving the office to meet friends and her evenings were taken up with a high social life. Surprisingly she did not lose her job, which probably reflected an above average working ability when well. Her elation responded each time to lithium and it seemed likely that it would prevent a recurrence. After two months or so she would stop the treatment and not return to the clinic. She rejected the idea that the elation might recur and adamantly refused to meet other patients with this illness or attend group therapy sessions. She would say that 'there is nothing wrong with me—I'm just a bit run down. I'll just have to take it easy for a while'. At a later stage she angrily accused the hospital staff of trying to ruin her life and said that she did not consider it any of their concern what might happen to her in the future.

Along the way patients will go through a stage of apparent indifference, followed by, to a greater or lesser degree, a hostile dismissal of the illness and its implications until they finally come to terms with its reality. For some, this point of rational understanding is achieved in a matter of weeks, while others have to travel the hard road of personal experience before they can truly come to terms with the illness. This was what happened to Marcia. Three years later and after further hospitalisations she realised that her approach was not working. She eventually began to listen to other patients with similar experiences who had come to accept the illness. They helped her to see the pattern of her mood swings, and how to avail herself of the treatments necessary to achieve stability. Marcia is one of the lucky ones—she still has a job and a family to return to. Others who have taken as long to reach acceptance have had to suffer irredeemable losses.

Those with recurrent depressive mood swings are able to accept the need for continuing preventive treatment as they know the pain of depression and dread its return. This contrasts with those who have bouts of elation. They miss their highs, regard them as very productive periods and they cannot imagine how they could manage with less energy. Usually they have not assessed the full range of effects associated with elation. The first of these is that they will probably have depression after the elation. The so-called productive periods tend to be more illusionary than real. Often when a person has gone back and accurately assessed his work done during an elation he comes to realise how his perception was distorted by the mood, and what he thought was a job well done was anything but. Finally, they need to get their families' and friends' views if they are in any doubt about the adverse effects of their elation.

A true acceptance can only be gained by having factual information about the illness. This, more than anything else, will help dispel the irrational fears which are so much part of any mental illness. So, let those parts of your mind which do not want to hear have the facts. Likewise, have some family member or close friend understand it with you. It is important that you both have the one perception of your mood swings. Taking an interest in the treatment, confiding in your doctor about nagging worries, and discussing your experiences with family members lightens the burden all round. Meeting fellow patients who have responded well to treatment always has a profound influence; they, more than anybody else, know what it is all about and will be able to point you in the right direction. So if you have the opportunity to meet such people who are now in the fortunate position to share their experience with you, do avail yourself of it.

6

Mood Swings and the Family

At the beginning of this book we heard the plaintive pleas of a patient and relative striving to bridge the gulf of misunderstanding which so often is a part of mood swings. Both were fixed in their views and blind to the other's position. Using the facts from the foregoing pages let us see how they can overcome their differences and achieve a realistic perspective of the illness.

Mood swings are a disorder of emotions and so the emotional bond between the patient and family will be altered in most instances during the illness. The depressed person who becomes withdrawn and quiet often shows little interest in family matters, and those around are often puzzled by his constant complaints of tiredness. He may both show little affection and be unable to feel the usual warm emotions of the immediate family. Mistakenly, he may interpret this as a real lack of interest by his spouse rather than a dulling of his own feelings because of depression. Marital conflict is the inevitable outcome. When tiredness is mistaken for laziness, inability to cope for irresponsibility, and lack of affection for indifference, family conflict is likely. With increasing depression the person suffering mood swings will be unable to fulfil his usual duties, placing a further burden on the family. However, at this stage the depression will be self-evident and the family will generally rally around.

For the family, elation is even more trying with its impossible demands, insensitive manner, and incessant activity. Worse still is the reckless spending and numerous attractions which steal the person away from home. Much of this behaviour, particularly in the teenage years, will be seen as badness or immaturity and evokes a hostile response from the family, often to the total bewilderment of the patient. When the family can accept that the patient's behaviour is part of an illness some sense of order is brought to a chaotic situation. The hurtful remarks, uncaring ways and wayward ideas can then be understood.

As helpful as this illness perspective is, relatives find it hard to relate to the changing moods. To begin with, they will have detached themselves emotionally for their own protection from the hurt of the elation and depression. As the mood swing subsides they will again re-establish their former relationships and accept the patient back into his usual role within the family. With each mood swing family members will be slower to leave the detached state and gradually the patient can find himself isolated from the family and living in a cocoon of his own, devoid of responsibilities.

This gradual drift from the family does not go unchecked. At first, concerned family members will encourage the patient to seek help, they will take an interest in his treatment and be willing to invest their time and emotions in doing what they can. Sometimes these are frantic attempts, born of a guilty conscience and so doomed to failure. But as time passes they lose heart in the face of prolonged or frequent mood swings. Other family members never get this far; they cannot accept the stigma of mental illness and in a state of guilt, imagined fears, or dread of what the future may hold never put words on their thoughts and feelings. They never attain a realistic grasp of the problem.

Fortunately, many can sustain the changing moods, stay by the patient's side and come through it all without being unduly hurt. Let us see how this might be achieved.

Advice for patients

This illness can be almost as trying for your family as for you. They just cannot ignore your plight even if you would wish it and if at times they appear to do so it is the only way that they can manage, what for them, is a perplexing and intangible illness.

Encourage them to get involved, tell them how your treatment is progressing, and endeavour to pass on the information you are gathering about the illness. Your doctor will certainly want to talk to them, initially to get an objective account of the mood swings and later to have an accurate assessment of your mood. The following account is a good example of the importance of a relative's role. Mary had a number of depressive mood swings, two of which resulted in hospitalisation despite her being on appropriate preventive treatment. She did not describe any periods of elation and even when questioned in detail about the symptoms of elation none was forthcoming. Her doctor was particularly interested in this aspect of her mood swings as he suspected that the reason her anti-depressant medication was ineffective was that it was intensifying her mood swings. Her husband was reluctant to travel to hospital to provide an objective history and she, for other reasons, was not keen that he be interviewed. With some persuasion both consented to a meeting. When questioned he gave a clear-cut account of a spurt of activity, overtalkativeness, and great spirits in the month preceding each depression. Evidently the elation was precipitated by the anti-depressants and the mood swing then followed its usual course to a depression. As expected, when her treatment was changed to lithium the mood swings were well controlled.

Remember that elation can steal up on you and those with whom you are living will often be the first to notice the change. Provided there is a family member in whom you have been able to confide and who has a factual understanding of the illness they are ideally placed to encourage you to take appropriate steps. Those who do not have a relative or friend to help out often find that the elation goes undetected until hospital admission is inevitable. Similarly, your doctor will be happier to treat the mood swings without resorting to hospitalisation, but often will be only able to do so if he knows that there is a supportive and caring relative in the background. In practice, this, more than the severity of the mood swing, will determine whether a person who is moderately depressed or elated is going to be treated in hospital or at home. This relative needs to be able to gauge the severity of the mood, be aware of the complications which may occur and be given the full cooperation of the patient. Two brief case histories will make this point.

John had noticed that for a few nights in a row he was having trouble getting to sleep, that he was overtalkative and was more lively than usual. He had mentioned it to his wife who confirmed his impression, and they went to see his doctor. From previous experience his doctor knew that John and his wife spoke freely about their problems, were able to manage the medication and make appropriate adjustments as the elation subsided. Therefore he was happy to prescribe medication and review the position later.

Brian, on the other hand, with much the same degree of elation, tended to hide the signs from his wife, usually underestimated its severity, took medication erratically, and on his last elation accumulated a large bank overdraft. He arrived at his doctor's surgery two weeks later in a highly elated state and had to be admitted to hospital.

The ideal situation is when your doctor and close relatives have the same perspective of the illness and can communicate freely with each other. This means that you must be prepared to relinquish some control to your family. Telling them that you want them to intervene in whatever way they think appropriate should you become elated again, or to manage your pills during a depression, gives them a sense of control over events, makes them less apprehensive and thus less restrictive in their approach.

As you recover from a mood change your family will be just as apprehensive as you about a future relapse; keeping them informed about how you are feeling and about your visits to the doctor will lessen their anxieties. Jane, at first, did otherwise. She felt that since she got over her last depression her mother was watching her every move, always looking for a sign of a mood swing. When she was out late at night or played her records loudly she was considered to be elated, and if she stayed in bed in the morning she was asked if she was depressed. Jane responded to all of this by becoming secretive and avoided conversation with her mother. Obviously her mother was over-reacting but what Jane had overlooked was that she was very concerned. Both complained about each other to the doctor. After discussing the problem Jane agreed to be more open about her feelings and give her mother some information about her visits to the doctor. Her mother undertook not to question her movements and to be more relaxed in her approach. Within weeks their relationship improved and Jane's mother saw her as being capable and in control. Obviously her anxiety had been dealt with by her daughter.

If you think your family cannot understand how you feel and despair of any change ask yourself whether your attitude would be any different if positions were reversed. Listen to their advice, talk out the hurtful things which were said or occurred during the mood swing and, most of all, allow time for a healing of the strained relationships.

Advice for families

Guilt and fear of the unknown are probably the twin factors which limit an understanding of mood swings. Hopefully the foregoing pages will have dispelled these misplaced emotions. Your help is vital for a successful outcome and for limiting the complications. However, it is essential to be guided by the patient in this respect. Initially, particularly during elation, he may resent your involvement. If you wait too long to get medical help you may have a number of complications to cope with, so it is best not to delay. If the patient is reluctant to listen to your advice then try to get him to talk to another relative or close friend who might be heeded. Should this fail it is advisable to ask your doctor to intervene. With time, patients usually come to accept the need for a relative's participation. However, it is essential that the particular relative or friend has a factual understanding of the pattern of the illness, its signs and symptoms, and is able to detect early symptoms of mood change.

As your understanding and sense of familiarity of the illness grows, much of the stress involved will lessen. Liaising between doctor and patient is a particularly important function. Sometimes you may have to detach temporarily when things get too much, particularly when, despite your best efforts, the patient has to be hospitalised. Don't feel guilty because of this—it does not mean that you have failed. At times like these, meeting other patients' relatives who have been through similar crises can be a comfort. They will help you cope with this burden, sometimes by simply being able to identify with your problems, and other times by giving you the benefit of their experience. As Paul's wife put it: 'I thought I was the only one with this problem. I really didn't know what was wrong. I thought he might have been drinking too much. And he used to blame me for everything.' Gradually she realised that her husband had an illness and that neither she nor he were to blame. With this in mind, she became more constructive in her approach to the problem and took an active part in aiding his recovery. Organisations such as the Manic-Depression Association and the Mood Disorder Fellowship hold meetings for patients with recurrent mood swings and their relatives. These provide essential information and emotional support for those who are finding it difficult to cope with the emotional strain of the illness. Your family doctor or Social Services Department will be able to tell you about the support services in your locality.

With recurrent mood swings you or one of the family may have to take over the patient's former role within the family and general responsibilities. This may involve making all the major decisions, ensuring that there is sufficient money and generally managing the family affairs. When the patient has been discharged from hospital and the mood has stabilised you will be understandably apprehensive about the future and may find it easier to cope by continuing with your new responsibilities. This will leave the patient isolated within the family, devoid of responsibilities and—sometimes lacking a sense of purpose in life—they lose their self-respect. If there has been a trusting and confiding relationship throughout the illness your anxiety about returning control to the patient will be less. Sean's story shows what can go wrong. He had a long history of mood swings which had a disruptive effect on his family. His wife, Ann, was supportive throughout, and went out to work when Sean lost his job. The older children played their part by helping with the housework and taking on some responsibilities which previously would have been dealt with by their father. When eventually Sean made a stable recovery he found his family had passed him by. His daughter became used to telling him what to do, his wife left him on his own a lot as she was busy with her work. He felt he was still being treated as if he was depressed and that he had lost the respect of his wife and family. Only after many arguments and scenes were they able to make room for him again. He also had to be patient and understanding about their fears of a further relapse.

The different approaches you will have to adopt with the changing moods are probably the most trying aspects of the illness. However, approaching the problems in a commonsense way and heeding the advice I have set out in the various sections will see you through. As the patient's mood stabilises and they begin to accept the need for a continuously preventive approach you will see your patience and understanding being fully rewarded.

7

Some Common Questions

Are mood swings common?

Mood swings occur more commonly than is generally realised. Let us first look at the frequency of depression as a whole. Various community surveys show that about 17 per cent of the population at any one time have depressive symptoms and, on average, 7 per cent have sufficiently more persistent and upsetting symptoms to warrant a diagnosis of depressive illness. Much of this depression is probably not recognised—fewer than half of those detected in community surveys had actually attended their doctor with the problem.

It is estimated that some 3 per cent of men and 6 per cent of women get depressive mood swings. About 1 per cent of the population can expect to have a mood swing of elation and depression at some point in their lives. Although these figures make manic depression a relatively rare condition it is likely that it occurs more frequently than this. When we recall that mild to moderate elation often goes unnoticed and that the person may only be aware of the accompanying depression, it would not be wildly speculative to suppose that elation is much more common than is at first apparent.

At what age do mood swings start?

Mood swings tend to occur for the first time between the teenage years and the forties with the average age of onset being thirty years. However, it is not unknown for mania to start in later life.

In the early teenage years elation and depression are often overlooked. At that time of life the person often lacks the repertoire of emotional experiences to describe how he is feeling, particularly when the mood change has been gradual. Furthermore, much of his behavioural change will be attributed to the teenage problems of growing up. Mood swings in children are even more difficult to diagnose. Whereas mild depression is not an uncommon experience in the early formative years, cycles of elation and depression are rare before puberty. However, childhood elation has been reported.

In general, women are twice as likely to suffer from depression as men, but this difference is much less marked for manic depression. Some authorities claim that there is no real difference between the sexes in this respect and that the slightly lower prevalence rate in men reflects the fact that a number of men with mood swings have developed alcohol problems, and thus their mood disorder is never recognised as such.

Is personality a factor?

Relatives are usually puzzled when the person first has a mood swing, commenting that the individual always had been normal in every way—'steadfast, reliable, a real tower of strength, the last person you would expect this to happen to'. However, some report that the person always tended to be moody; for weeks they would be in exceptionally good form, full of the joys of spring, and then they would become quiet and irritable. These mild highs and lows are referred to as a 'cyclothymic personality type'. Others are described as being persistently exuberant, lively, energetic and more dynamic than most. A third type noticed are those with rigid attitudes and perfectionistic habits. These traits are more often associated with those who get recurrent depressions. All of these personality types are also found among those who never had a mental illness and are not just confined to those who develop mood swings.

Personality and mood swings can interact in another way. How a person copes with a mood swing is in some respect dependent on his character. While some are determined to carry on despite a depressive swing, a less robust individual may crumble with the same intensity of depression. Elation, too, has a way of magnifying any personality foible. Those who are usually less observant than most about society's standards and values will often be even more so during an elation and so are more likely to get involved in irregular and illicit deeds.

Will I be able to control the elation if it happens again?

Presuming that you have spotted the elation in its early stages you will still be in a position to take some action. At this point it is best that you discuss the change with one of the family and call on your doctor. With their help and the medication the doctor prescribes you will, in most instances, remain in control of the mood swing.

79

If you are elated it is dangerous to go it alone. Even if the mood change is mild it is advisable to check its degree with somebody who is likely to be more objective. It is not unusual for a person to think that they can control their thoughts and behaviour when elated. While avoiding detailed discussions, having periods alone to help you relax and forgoing social gatherings will help limit the elation, you may not be able to institute these. Once an elation or depression intensifies will-power and determination will be of little use and they should never be your only defence.

Surely depression is due to the social pressures of Western society?

No culture is immune to depression and most surveys show that rates of depression do not differ greatly between cultures or between races. While figures which refer to the number who were treated for depression show mood disorders to be more prevalent in Western societies, this data cannot be interpreted as substantiating a real difference in the overall frequency of depression between cultures. Some 50 per cent of those with depression in our own community do not seek medical help and it is easy to see how this percentage would be increased in a society with lesser treatment facilities and with different attitudes to mental illness and how it should be managed.

Culture does, however, influence the way a depression might exhibit itself. Some cultures do not have the term 'depression' in their vocabulary. This does not mean that they do not experience 'depression' as we understand it, but that they perceive and express it differently. For example, *susto* or 'soul-loss', a disorder characterised by the sudden onset of weakness, loss of appetite, sleep disturbance, fear, anxiety and markedly reduced physical and mental activity is quite common in Central and South America. As you can see this description is quite like a Western-type depression although it is not referred to as such.

Guilt, suicidal thoughts and self-condemnatory remarks are rarely experienced by depressed patients in parts of Africa and India, but in areas of these continents which have been Western-ised such symptoms are commonly encountered. In Arab cultures abdominal pain, weight loss and constipation are major features of depression and, again, guilt feelings and self-destructive tend-encies are unusual. Why should Western depressions have self-blame as a prominent symptom? One suggestion is that it results

80

from the great emphasis Western cultures place on the person's productivity and accomplishments so that, when depression disrupts these, guilt feelings emerge. In societies that are less demanding in this respect the depressed person will not tend to view his incapacity as a form of personal failure.

How will I know when my mood is normal?

This question is frequently put by those who have been having recurrent mood swings for a number of weeks or months and feel they have forgotten what normality is like. The simple answer is that they will recognise it when they are there and the objective signs of elation and depression, which I have described, will be absent.

While some patients find it hard to accept illness and ignore the early signs of a relapse, others, particularly when they first come to see the need to be vigilant, are over-cautious and question every change in feeling. Remember to rely on how you feel during depression and on what you are doing during elation to spot the onset of a mood swing. If, for example, you have had trouble getting off to sleep for three consecutive nights and do not feel tired on the following day then you are probably heading for an elation. On the other hand, if, with the same degree of sleepless-ness, you feel tired and know that your sleep difficulty is due to a change in shift duty, then it is unlikely that your mood is changing.

How could I feel depressed at a time when my doctor says I'm elated?

There are two ways in which a person can feel depressed during an elation. But first let me point out that when your doctor concludes that you are elated he is basing this on a range of objective signs and not just on your predominant feeling. This does not mean that he is ignoring the depression.

If you feel agitated, tense and depressed during an elation it probably means that your thoughts are racing faster than you can cope with. As with any distressing sensation such as pain, mental agitation often induces a type of reactive depression; in a sense it is your mind's way of saying it is fed up with the incessant barrage of thoughts. If your doctor were to treat these symptoms as a depression the agitation would in fact worsen. When the standard

81

anti-elatant medication is increased these distressing feelings disappear.

The other possible explanation for such depressed feelings is that the person is responding in an emotionally appropriate manner to some upsetting incident of personal significance. Not infrequently, in elation, a person's emotional responses are heightened and what otherwise might not be a bother, now calls forth tears and a type of exalted sadness.

Will tablets limit what I can do?

When you first start treatment for an acute elation or depression you will probably have some side-effects, but these are usually minimal. They may, however, hinder your ability to perform your usual chores, drive a car or participate in some recreational activities. Usually you will soon experience the benefits of treatment and will be able to tolerate these inconveniences until the medication begins to take effect.

If you need to have an ongoing preventive treatment the side-effects should be negligible. Your doctor, when prescribing lithium or anti-depressants, will be anxious to ensure that you have no side-effects. Should you have unwanted effects from medication do let him know as they can usually be overcome by reducing the dosage or changing to an alternative treatment. If, despite these changes, there is no lessening of the effects, then both you and your doctor will have to decide whether to stop the medication and run the risk of a relapse and all that goes with it, or continue with the treatment. Most patients have a clear view of the overall benefits which these medications confer and are happy to persist with treatment.

It is not intended that continuous preventive medication should in any way interfere with a person's work or leisure activities. Artists, surgeons, jewellers, pilots, writers, athletes, golfers and mountaineers can all continue to pursue their interests whether they require precision and manual dexterity or ingenuity and creativity.

What do I tell our children about the illness?

Younger children will ask the questions they want answered when they are ready. You and your spouse can help them to best understand the mood swings by creating the right environment to enable them to ask these questions. If they hear you, as parents, openly discussing the facts about the mood swings, see you going for your visits to the doctor or taking pills, they will develop an easy familiarity with it and will want their curiosity satisfied. On the other hand, if they hear you speaking in a hushed tone about the problem, see you hiding the medication or generally being secretive they will feel awkward, be reluctant to probe and may develop all sorts of imagined fears about the problem. So creating the right environment is more dependent on your own attitude to the illness than how you might explain it. When your child asks, give a simple but honest reply to their specific question rather than a detailed account of all the aspects of the problem. They will return with further queries if they are not satisfied. For teenagers a further discussion is necessary as they will be very aware of the impact of the mood swings on relationships within the family. Again, they will tend to adopt whatever attitude you and your husband have no matter what you may say to the contrary.

Why do I get paranoid when I am elated?

Paranoid or suspicious thoughts are a frequent occurrence in both phases of a mood swing. Some people are more prone to these than others and it probably means that they have a greater tendency than average to be mistrustful by nature even when well.

In depression the usual guilt feelings are very real to the patient. He is so convinced that his ineptitude or wrongdoing has substance that he will look for confirmatory signs in what others say about him. He will listen and watch so intently for these signs that he can come to believe that people are talking about him and that because of his imagined misdeeds he will be punished.

The process is different in elation. Here the hyperactive mind seems to need to make sense of everything. As a result trivial and incidental happenings are incorrectly connected in the patient's mind often leading to a variety of paranoid beliefs. An example of this is where one person while elated was woken at 4 p.m. by a loud bang coming from the street. When he went out onto the street he saw a bearded man standing at a nearby bus stop. He concluded that this man was trying to kill him as he thought that the noise he heard was an attempt to explode a bomb which had misfired. When his elation subsided he could see how ridiculous the idea was and knew from previous elations that he was always suspicious when 'high'.

If I avoid stress will I prevent another mood swing?

Most mood swings are not preceded by stressful events, at least not of a significant kind. As this illness tends to run in families and has been shown by twin and adoption research to be mainly of biological origin we can see how emotionally distressing happenings cannot be the main cause of this type of mood disorder. However, this does not mean that stress is irrelevant. What can be said is that before a mood swing of depression or elation a person may well be going through more than the usual day-to-day problems but that the same degree of stress would not be sufficient to produce a mood swing in somebody without the same genetic liability. So avoiding what one would consider to be the 'normal' problems of living is not going to prevent a mood swing and even if it did it could hardly be a feasible approach.

A small proportion of those who have recurrent moods always have either a definite disappointment or are faced with some daunting task beforehand. They cope well with life's average problems and are only affected by more imposing events. It would seem that they have a lower biological tendency towards mood swings than most who develop it, and their genetic liability will only be apparent when they are grossly overburdened with problems. Avoiding major stress will obviously be an essential part of their treatment plan. This would mean asking the person concerned about the type of events that are particularly associated with his mood swings and how much control he has over the occurrence of these events. Some of the stressful situations he experiences will have been of his own doing and he may be repeating his mistakes. Psychotherapy will help to identify these emotional blind spots so that the person will understand his actions in terms of hidden unconscious motives. For a person whose mood swings are stress related this may involve accepting that there are certain demands which he places on himself to achieve that which is beyond his capability; and so he may need to modify his approach to life. Obviously it is impossible to prevent all problems as many will not be within his control, but when they happen their traumatic effect can be lessened by discussing his feelings with a close relative or friend. This helps to defuse an accumulation of distressful emotions.

Would genetic counselling tell which of my children might get mood swings?

Our understanding of how mood swings are inherited is extremely sketchy. While we know that the mode of transmission within a family is largely genetic, the way the gene is carried and transmitted is unknown. The genetic mistake may be carried by one or several genes or, what seems more likely, there may be several different types of faulty genes any of which can produce the same signs and symptoms; in other words, there probably are different genetic types of mood swings. All of this makes predicting the probability of mood problems in a particular patient's offspring precarious. If, on the other hand, we knew that there was one gene responsible for mood swings and understood what type of gene this was, accurate predictions would be possible. This is the case, for example, with cystic fibrosis, an inherited disorder affecting the lungs and absorption of food from the bowel. It is possible to predict accurately how many offspring will be affected depending on whether one or both· parents are affected.

Realising the limitations of genetic counselling, let us see how the risk for relatives is calculated. The rate of mood swings detected among relatives of a large group of patients is the starting point. Various surveys show that about 15 per cent of the close relatives (fathers, mothers, brothers, sisters, children) of patients with mood swings will also have them. However, this figure cannot be directly applied to an individual patient's relatives. The geneticist will then, on the basis of a detailed study of the frequency and pattern of mood disorders in your family over three generations, calculate the particular risk. For example, if the rate of mood disorders is lower for your family than the average for other patients with this disorder then the risk for your relatives will be less than the 15 per cent average. This type of prediction is at best approximate and does not allow for other factors such as the effect of unpredictable environmental influences or that of genes inherited from the other parent.

It is not possible to predict which, if any, of your offspring will develop mood swings. Finally, I must emphasise that, just because there is a hereditary basis for mood disorders, this does not mean that they cannot be treated. In fact, research evidence indicates that those with a definite family history of depression and elation are more likely to respond favourably to lithium than those without a family tendency.

A Summary of the Do's and Don'ts

Remember that mood swings are treatable.

Learn all you can about your illness—its symptoms, causes, complications and the range of available treatments. Being so informed will help you come to terms with it and enable you to get the maximum benefit from treatment.

Know about your tablets, their names, doses and possible or probable side-effects and why they are being prescribed.

If you have the opportunity to talk to those who have this illness, do so. It can be a great comfort to know how they have coped with their experiences and will help you to accept the possibility of having further mood swings.

If you notice that you are becoming depressed or elated don't pretend it is not happening. Early treatment will minimise the effect of the mood change and prevent complications. At such times avoid making major decisions or changes in your life.

Allow a relative to get involved with your treatment. Choose somebody in whom you can confide and who knows the facts about the illness. That person will be a great support to you during the mood swings, will help you make the right decisions and protect you from the hazards of the illness.

When you feel depressed keep active if possible—most find it uplifting if they can complete their daily routine or take some physical exercise. With a more severe depression such activity will be impossible and you will have to disengage from your usual pursuits until the anti-depressant treatment has had an effect.

During an elation be guided by your relatives and accept the restraints they may need to place on your activities. Avoid situations which you know from previous experience can lead to complications, for example, long trips away from home, parties, shopping, or getting involved in other people's problems.

Talk to the family—let them know how you are feeling and how

87

your treatment is progressing. When your mood has settled discuss the hurtful words and happenings of previous mood swings—don't just brush them aside.

Avoid alcohol. It can both depress and make the depression worse. Those with mood swings are particularly prone to become dependent on alcohol. It is best not to drink until the moods have been stabilised. Your doctor will advise you about the interactions between alcohol and any tablets you are taking.

Remember that the complications of elation and depression can be avoided. You and your family can do much to prevent them.

Lithium Advice Sheet

Know which lithium tablets you are taking and the prescribed dose.

Lithium should be taken in equal doses three to four times daily rather than just in the morning or evening. This will give a more even level of lithium in your body. It is not essential to take the tablets at *exactly* the same time each day but it is important to take the prescribed amount. A pill box, with a compartment for each of the day's doses, will help you remember to take them regularly.

When you are having a lithium blood test always ensure that it is taken 12 hours after the last lithium tablet.

Ask your doctor about your blood lithium level. If the level is below 0.5 millimoles per litre you are unlikely to benefit from the treatment. If it is greater than 1.3 millimoles per litre you will probably experience toxic effects.

The side-effects of lithium treatment are: tremor; polyuria (increased flow of urine) and polydypsia (increased intake of fluid); weight gain (usually due to high-calorie drinks taken to relieve thirst); acne; and goitre and hypothyroidism (swelling and underactivity of the thyroid gland in the neck). If you are experiencing any of these side-effects report them to your doctor. By reducing your blood lithium concentration he will be able to limit their effect.

Once your blood lithium concentration is at a satisfactory level and your mood has been stabilised it will only be necessary to have a blood test once every three months to check the lithium level, thyroid gland activity and kidney function.

The following may increase your blood lithium level:
vomiting; diarrhoea; profuse sweating (when the fluid and salt loss is not being replaced); slimming diets; reduced food intake during a mood swing; diuretics (water tablets); and kidney disease. In these circumstances the blood lithium will have to be monitored more frequently—so consult your doctor. If another doctor

prescribes tablets or a diet do tell him that you are taking lithium.

Women of child-bearing age who are taking lithium must take contraceptive precautions because of the risk of foetal damage. Lithium treatment is generally discontinued for the first three months of pregnancy. If you are planning to breastfeed your child you will have to stop taking lithium as it will otherwise be present in your milk.

Know the symptoms of lithium toxicity (blood lithium level greater than 1.3 mmol/1): drowsiness and weakness; nausea, vomiting and diarrhoea; marked tremor; slurred speech; and muscle twitching. Even if you only have one of these symptoms contact your doctor without delay.

Lithium, like all medicines, should be kept out of reach of children.

Don't stop taking the lithium just because you feel well— remember this treatment is being prescribed to prevent further mood swings. If you are concerned about continuing to take it, raise the question with your doctor.

Appendix 3

Admission to Hospital

Hospital care is often necessary at some stage of the illness. A severe depression with a suicidal potential or an elation which is rapidly becoming unmanageable in a patient who is still unaware of the mood change, will make entry to hospital a matter of urgency. Such admissions can be both life-saving and prevent many complications. Other, and less urgent, reasons for hospitalisation are the intensive treatment of resistant depression, observation of the patient's pattern of mood swings more closely than is possible on an out-patient basis, thus enabling the development of a personally tailored preventive treatment plan, and the adjustment of medications that have been causing side-effects. Occasionally patients are admitted for frequent blood lithium estimations, kidney function tests or for diagnostic hormonal investigations.

If you have never been to a psychiatric hospital or unit your perception of them will probably be quite different from their reality. Unfortunately their stereotyped image has not changed as rapidly as the advances in care and treatment which they have to offer. While the standards of care and accommodation vary between hospitals, most patients being admitted for the first time are pleasantly surprised by the range of treatment facilities and recreational activities which are part of a modern psychiatric hospital. The closed doors and personal restrictions with the emphasis on custodial care have been replaced by greater individual freedom and enlightened attitudes, making them centres of active treatment and specialised investigations.

The vast majority of patients who are now being admitted to psychiatric hospitals go of their own accord. Those admitted compulsorily are usually acutely disturbed, and most, on recovery, readily accept the necessity for their admission procedure. In fact many who were once hospitalised against their wishes often later seek voluntary admission, realising that they benefited from their stay. It is important to emphasise that compulsory admission does not mean that the period in hospital is going to be unduly prolonged. In fact, the average stay is probably no longer than that for a voluntary patient admitted with a similar problem, as the patient will be discharged once the doctor considers that he has recovered.

If the depression or elation becomes difficult to manage your doctor will recommend hospital treatment. While you may welcome the chance of a rest with constant nursing and medical care you are more likely to be frightened at the prospect of going to hospital. Discuss your apprehension with a relative or a friend and, if necessary, go to see the hospital before deciding against admission. Your doctor will explain what is involved, outline the admission and discharge procedures and inform you of your legal rights. When a person is seriously ill and is in urgent need of hospital treatment but refuses to seek voluntary admission, the family will have to consider compulsory hospitalisation. The procedure for this varies from country to country and your family doctor or community welfare officer will be able to give you the details and explain the legal safeguards.

When you go to the hospital you will have plenty of questions to ask. Doctors and nurses are well aware of how apprehensive people are at such times and they will do all they can to allay your fears—so do not hesitate to ask. Most hospitals will have a booklet which will tell you about the hospital and its facilities and give you details about visiting hours and recreational and therapeutic activities. Psychologists, social workers and occupational therapists will probably be involved in your care as they work as a team with doctors and nurses to look after your psychological and social needs.

A frequent worry for new patients is how they will get along with other patients. They may think that everybody else will be very disturbed or may fear being physically attacked. Naturally there will be some patients who will be worse than you are but also many who are almost fully recovered and awaiting discharge. You will, no doubt, meet people from similar backgrounds and with problems just like yours. After you have shed your initial fears you will find that you will make friends and be better able to participate in the daily activities. If you have cause to worry about other patients talk to the nurses and they will do all they can to help.

Relatives often feel ill at ease and unsure of what to say when they come to visit. Their fears are often similar to those of patients but, with time, they too will develop a sense of familiarity. They should keep visits short, particularly in the early stages, as the patient will probably find it hard to concentrate or engage in conversation when acutely distressed. A short visit is reassuring and will cater for the patients' needs without being too much of a burden. Sometimes a well-meaning visitor will talk about all that is happening at home or at work and in a sense bring the problems of the outside world to the patient. This can make it difficult for the patient to become fully involved in their treatment programme as they will feel they really ought to be elsewhere.

During a depressed mood the patient will be withdrawn, probably reluctant to talk and you will find it hard to make any impression on their mood. It is all too easy to find yourself despairing if the visit is prolonged. Endeavour to be cheerful, quietly encouraging, and ask them if you can be of any practical help. While seeing that their commitments are being looked after and arranging for certain visitors to call are useful, it is essential that you do not implement any of the decisions which they have made because of the depression. When elated, the patient will be distractable and may talk in a loud and uninhibited manner about confidential matters. In some instances they may blame you for their hospitalisation or implore you to arrange their discharge. You may well feel annoyed but it is best to avoid confrontations, remembering that they are ill and have limited control over their feelings. As with depression, it is advisable to avoid complying with the requests of an elated patient if you consider them likely to lead to complications.

As the patients' mood abates they will be encouraged to attend therapeutic activities which are designed both to educate them about their illness and to help them learn new ways of coping. Some hospitals will have organised lectures on a range of mental health issues and these can be of great value to those trying to understand the nature of their own illness and other psychiatric disorders. Group therapy, of which there are many types, forms an important part of most hospitals' treatment programmes. Here, participants are able to explore their feelings and attitudes with the help of fellow patients and a group therapist, identify their psychological blind spots and effect the changes which are necessary for their peace of mind. Many who attend the art or occupational therapy departments begin to appreciate the importance of a creative leisure activity which they will often continue with on returning home. Relaxation therapy, social skills and assertiveness training, and music and drama therapy are some of the therapeutic methods used in modern and progressive psychiatric hospitals. These multi-disciplinary therapies often have a major bearing on the patient's recovery, giving him new insight into his psychological make-up and helping to equip him with the necessary coping skills to face life anew.

With the ending of a depression or an elation will come thoughts of discharge. This often brings mixed feelings; on the one hand you will be looking forward to returning home but on the other you may be apprehensive and uncertain about meeting friends and neighbours again. What will they say, what will they think and how do I explain it all will be some of the thoughts uppermost in your mind. It is essential that you do not postpone returning home or, having been discharged, avoid meeting people. Going on weekend leave from hospital is a good way of being gradually reintroduced to the outside world as well as being a useful test of how well prepared you are for discharge. Remember that those whom you meet may feel just as awkward having to ask the inevitable questions and giving them a simple account of your hospitalisation is all that is necessary. In a week or so you probably will have met those who matter most and you will be able to get on with your life without referring to your illness.

When you are leaving hospital your doctor will tell you of what the future may hold and what to do if you are beginning to relapse. You will be advised about out-patient visits and, if necessary, about the need to continue with medication. If you have any questions do not hesitate to ask. Hopefully, your stay in hospital will not only have resulted in a successful treatment of your mood swing but will offer some guarantee of stability for the future.

Suggestions for Further Reading

The Brain, a *Scientific American* publication, San Francisco, W. H. Freeman and Co, 1979.

Brown, G. W. and Harris, T., *Social Origins of Depression*, London, Tavistock Publications, 1978.

Paykel, E. S., *Handbook of Affective Disorders*, London, Churchill Livingstone, 1982.

Weisman, M. M. and Paykel, E. S., *The Depressed Woman—A Study of Social Relationships*, Chicago, University of Chicago Press, 1974.

Winokur, G., *Depression: The Facts*, Oxford, Oxford University Press, 1981.

Index